The University of New Mexico
At Gallup

Zollinger Library

The Green
Workplace

The Green Workplace

SUSTAINABLE STRATEGIES THAT BENEFIT EMPLOYEES, THE ENVIRONMENT, AND THE BOTTOM LINE

Leigh Stringer, LEED® AP

Vice President, HOK

THE GREEN WORKPLACE
Copyright © HOK, Inc., 2009.
All rights reserved.

First published in 2009 by PALGRAVE MACMILLAN® in the United States–a division of St. Martin's Press LLC, 175 Fifth Avenue, New York, NY 10010.

Where this book is distributed in the UK, Europe and the rest of the world, this is by Palgrave Macmillan, a division of Macmillan Publishers Limited, registered in England, company number 785998, of Houndmills, Basingstoke, Hampshire RG21 6XS.

Palgrave Macmillan is the global academic imprint of the above companies and has companies and representatives throughout the world.

Palgrave® and Macmillan® are registered trademarks in the United States, the United Kingdom, Europe and other countries.

ISBN 978-0-230-61428-4

Library of Congress Cataloging-in-Publication Data
Stringer, Leigh.
    The green workplace : sustainable strategies that benefit employees, the environment, and the bottom line / Leigh Stringer.
        p.   cm.
    ISBN-13: 978-0-230-61428-4
    ISBN-10: 0-230-61428-0
    1. Industrial management—Environmental aspects.   2. Work environment.
3. Organizational change.   4. Sustainable development.   I. Title.
HD30.255.S77   2009
658.4'083—dc22

                                                                    2009006375

A catalogue record of the book is available from the British Library.

Design by Letra Libre, Inc.

First edition: August 2009
10   9   8   7   6   5   4   3   2   1
Printed in the United States of America.

To Kate . . . the littlest greeniac.

Contents

Tables and Figures

Tables

Figures

Preface

Can we save the environment without destroying our economy? Is the battle against global warming the path to a brighter financial future or to a new Great Depression? And how can an individual company take actions that not only help forge a greener future—but add more "green" to the bottom line as well?

With the global environment and the economy both in the midst of a period of great crisis, these questions have never been more relevant. And these are the questions this book aims to answer.

My own path to these questions came through my somewhat unusual job, one that combines cutting-edge architecture with bottom-line, practical business. I work for Hellmuth, Obata & Kassabaum, P.C. (HOK), one of the world's largest architectural firms and an established industry leader in sustainability, particularly regarding the built environment. At the end of 2008, HOK counted 853 Leadership in Energy and Environmental Design (LEED) accredited professionals, 216 LEED registered projects, 36 LEED certified projects, and 6 Building Research Establishment Environmental Assessment Method (BREEAM)–certified projects. LEED and BREEAM, in case you are unfamiliar with these acronyms, are third party rating systems that define "green buildings" by a common standard of measurement. They consider a wide variety of environmental considerations including energy, material and water use, the health and well-being of building occupants, emissions, operational policies, land use, and the building's effect on local ecology. Luckily for me, I work for a company with experts in building design, urban planning, landscape design, engineering, and sustainable design, who all scurry in to work every day to dream up new ways to design and build more sustainably. I sit on the board of directors at HOK and am one of the leaders of HOK Advance Strategies, a consulting practice that works with clients before design starts to ensure that our clients are making the right workplace and real-estate decisions to support their business missions and their employees.

I was trained as an architect but also earned my MBA, as I have always had an interest in business. But, to be honest, I have not always been passionate about the environment. In architecture school, I was pretty oblivious to "green" issues. I still remember one of my professors chastising me on one of my first projects: "You think just because you used wood on this building that it's 'natural?' The material you chose has to be heavily treated with chemicals, put on a truck and shipped 2,000 miles to get to the job site. That's not exactly environmentally friendly!"

Only in the last few years did I experience what I call an "environmental enlightenment," in the sense that I became concerned about our impact as humans on the planet. I have, in part, Al Gore to thank for this. I went to see his movie, *An Inconvenient Truth,* shortly after it came out in 2006. The film really struck me, and it got me thinking about the impact of our collective environmental problems on the economy, our health, and the lifestyle to which we've become accustomed. Of course, I also have my daughter Kate to thank. Her birth—right around the time *An Inconvenient Truth* was released—suddenly made the idea of "future generations" much more than a mere abstraction. It really highlighted the reality that many years of disregard for the earth's natural systems would impact not just me, but my children and my children's children.

In July 2007, I was asked to speak in Orlando, Florida at the American Institute of Architects (AIA) Florida state convention about sustainability and the workplace. Although I have a passion for both subjects, it wasn't until I started to weave them together into a presentation that I realized how little had been written about the two together. In November, a few months later, I used my research materials to start a blog called TheGreenWorkplace.com. The blog now has over two dozen content experts contributing stories about environmental issues and workplace trends of the day.

I have learned a great deal writing and editing this blog. Blogging requires regular writing and a blog left "unfed" for more than a day or two loses web traffic and public interest quickly. Because blogging is so "exposed"—anyone on the planet with an Internet connection can instantaneously see and react to what is being published—comments made by visitors to the site provided thoughtful counterpoints to our posts that immediately tested our assumptions. Having several people writing on the same subject in one place also gave focus to our collective research. Each of the writers has favorite Web sites, news feeds, and other sources of information that are brought to bear in the research and writing. In a way, TheGreenWorkplace.com has become a living research mechanism, as much of our work was enhanced over time through comments and "updates" to posts.

While I am still blogging, I have also been busily working with HOK specialists—as well as clients and partners—to understand what it means to be green in the workplace. This work, and a continuing interest in and passion for an ever-changing and fascinating subject, have inspired the content of this book.

I believe that our environmental challenges—our dependence on non-renewable energy, the toxic emissions we create that affect the air we breathe and our atmosphere, the diminishing supply of potable water, the increasing amount of waste we create, just to name a few—are some of the most complex and important problems of our time, but they won't be solved out of the kindness of our hearts. Sustainable strategies that are themselves "sustainable" are those that save money or make our lives easier in some way—preferably both. For example, take getting to work. Driving to work not only depletes non-renewable resources and creates carbon dioxide emissions, but also requires buying a car, paying license and registration fees, car maintenance and regular tune-ups, making frequent trips to the gas station, and paying parking fees and insurance. Walking or biking to work eliminates the financial and time burden of owning a car and saves you a trip to the gym.

Especially in times of financial uncertainty, environmentally friendly thinking makes a great deal of sense. It's about being frugal and preserving the limited resources we have on this planet. But, for me, it's more than that. As a working mother with way too much on her plate, I really value strategies and tools that make my life simpler, not more complicated. The concept of sustainability is more than an environmental concept in my view. It's about upholding a work style and lifestyle that I can manage and my family and friends can accept.

After countless exhausting business trips, I dream of a future in which I travel less, see my family more, exercise regularly, eat better, and work fewer hours. With this in mind, I've made many changes to my own life and work style, and have committed to making more. My team often works from home, which allows us all to commute less and perform concentrative tasks more efficiently. I walk to work when I don't have carpool duty, I eat organic and fresh foods when I can, and I reduce-reuse-recycle significantly more than I have in the past. But in the grand scheme of things both "doable" and increasingly essential, these changes only represent the beginning of the changes that can and should be made.

So much of the media today focuses on the "doom and gloom" of climate change. This book is about doing something about it. *The Green Workplace* presents hundreds of environmentally friendly strategies that one can adopt immediately as an individual, a team, or an organization. Not all of the strategies in this book will be appropriate for you, but you are sure to find a few relevant ideas that you can adopt tomorrow. Many of them are easy to do and will save money at the same time.

I wish you pleasant travels on your green journey.

Leigh Stringer
January 2009
Washington, D.C.

Acknowledgments

Although my name is on the cover of this book, there were many people involved with researching, writing, and editing its contents. A special thanks to the members of the HOK Advance Strategies team in Washington, D.C.—Jodi Williams, Claire Whitehill, Todd Pedersen, Edmund Velasco, Daphne Kiplinger, and Danielle Caylor—all of whom not only helped to write and research for this book, but provided moral support. I am eternally grateful for their hard work. Thanks to many other HOK colleagues who helped connect me to brilliant subject matter experts and provided content support including Mary Ann Lazarus, Anica Landreneau, Bill Valentine, Lauren Gibbs, Gerald Callo, Steve Hargis, Emily Golembiewski, Emma Wharton, Jennifer Mannier, John Reid, Kim Vinson, Steve Parshall, Nikki Duffner, Mike Plotnick, and John Gilmore. Thanks to my agent, Lauren Abramo, and to Palgrave Macmillan for investing in me and vastly improving the message of this book. And the biggest thanks of all goes to this book's toughest editors—my parents, Jim and Mary Helen Stringer, and my husband John Hlinko.

And finally, the following HOK clients and partners offered tremendous insights and lessons learned that not only provided real-life stories for this book, but also helped me to become a better consultant and a more environmentally aware person in the process.

- Craig Arnold, Real Estate, Building Projects Americas, BMW
- Jeff Austin, Vice President, Corporate Real Estate, Wachovia Bank
- Frank Bick, Executive Vice President, The Bick Group
- Jay Boren, Grants Associate, Google.org

- Valerie Casey, Leader, Digital Experiences Practice, IDEO and Founder, the Designers Accord
- Tim Dick, LEED AP, Director of Engineering, Foulger-Pratt Management, Inc.
- David Dunn, Real Estate, Director of Global Planning and Design, Nortel
- Julie Garden, Cisco United Kingdom
- Adam Giagni, Drama Development, Sony Pictures Entertainment
- Andy Hammond, Programme and Project Management, the WPP Group
- Judith Heerwagen, Founder, PhD, J.H. Heerwagen Associates
- Chris Hood, Program Manager, the HP Workplace, Hewlett Packard
- Don Horn, Director of Sustainable Design, General Services Administration
- Peter Johnson, Senior Vice President, Regional Manager for Washington, D.C., Boston Properties
- Kevin Kampschroer, Acting Director, Office of Federal High-Performance Green Buildings, General Services Administration
- Kevin Kelly, AIA, Senior Architect, Work Space Delivery Program, General Services Administration, Public Building Service
- Omar Khan, Google.org, PhD candidate, Department of Computer Science and Berkeley Institute of Design, University of California, Berkeley
- Randy Knox, Senior Director of Global Facilities and Real Estate, Adobe Systems Inc.
- Alicia Martin, Sustainability Manager, Sprint Enterprise Real Estate
- Bonnie D. Morrison, CPM, Executive Vice-President, Foulger-Pratt Management, Inc.
- Melissa Perlman, Manager of Public Relations, Office Depot
- Curtis Ravenel, Head of Global Sustainability Initiatives, Bloomberg
- Randy Salzman, Writer and Transportation Activist
- Meeta Shingne, Manager, Real Estate, the WPP Group
- Shannon Sentman, Attorney, Holland & Knight
- Yalmaz Siddiqui, Director of Environmental Strategy, Office Depot

- Rod Stevens, Architect/Facility Information Manager, Pioneer Hi-Bred, a DuPont business
- Sandy Thomaes, Senior Consultant, Corporate Real Estate, Canadian financial institution
- Paul Westbrook, Sustainable Development Manager, Texas Instruments

CHAPTER 1

The Case for Change

The future has a way of arriving unannounced.

—George Will, conservative American newspaper columnist,
journalist, and author

Tony Jones was having another crazy day at the office. The truth is, if he was being honest, he would tell you that nearly every day is pretty crazy. With his kids' ballet practices, soccer matches, and one client meeting after another, he has virtually no time to relax. He had thought that after years of working hard for the large multinational Alpha Inc., moving up the company ladder and dragging his family across the country, he would finally reap the rewards. And to an outside observer, it would seem that he had. Last year he had moved into a gorgeous new six-bedroom home in the suburbs with a three-car garage. He had just been promoted to senior vice president, received a hefty raise, and moved into a plush corner office with stunning views of the downtown skyline. He had dreamed about climbing to this level since he started with Alpha as an intern, sitting at a tiny desk crammed into the mailroom.

But in fact, to Tony, the rewards didn't seem terribly "rewarding." He felt rushed and harried and, frankly, unhappy. And that beautiful new office?

He hardly had the chance to even sit down in it. His day typically went something like this:

6:00 a.m.	Wake up, check e-mail and try desperately to get through the backlog.
7:00 a.m.	Throw on a suit and drive the kids to school.
8:15 a.m.	Stop by Starbucks for coffee and a bagel—to be wolfed down while driving.
8:30 a.m.	Arrive at the office and check e-mail.
9:30 a.m.	Print copies of reports for the next meeting.
10:00 a.m.	Meet with his team in a conference room to discuss an upcoming 10-day trip to Singapore.
Noon	Grab a sandwich, to be consumed between three conference calls.
1:30 p.m.	Check e-mail.
2:00 p.m.	Attend two more meetings that had to happen this week because of the Singapore trip.
5:00 p.m.	Write, think, and create new business ideas.
6:00 p.m.	Drive to the gym for a quick workout.
7:15 p.m.	Grab a fast-food dinner, to be eaten on the long ride home.
8:30 p.m.	Arrive back home, just in time to read bedtime stories to the kids.
9:30 p.m.	Read more e-mail.
11:00 p.m.	Watch the evening news and go to sleep.

Every day, Tony spends about three hours in his car and five to six hours attending meetings, writing e-mails, or participating in conference calls. He also spends significant amounts of time working through the logistics for his business travel with his coworkers and family. The ugly truth is that he only spends about two hours each day on the "real work" he is being paid big bucks to do. He feels guilty about this but doesn't see an alternative. Tony is proud of his job, but regrets that he does not have more time to spend with his family. These days, he tells himself, business moves fast and you have to move faster—even to the point of exhaustion—to keep up.

Although Tony does not often think about environmental issues, he is worried about the current financial crisis and the impact of higher gas prices on his long commute. Even for an executive, filling the tank a few times a week really adds up. His wife is worried about the impact of working late nights and traveling long distances on Tony's health, given his stress and chronic high blood pressure. Every once in a while, when he allows himself a moment to daydream about a different lifestyle, Tony wonders how his old coworker Greg Smith is doing in his new job.

A year ago, Greg left his position at Alpha Inc. to start a new career with a small environmental firm, Green Corp. Though taking this job with a smaller, less-established company carried some financial risk, staying at his old job would have carried an even greater risk. Because of all the travel required by that job—he had circled the globe twice and visited thirteen countries in just twelve months—he often went weeks at a time without seeing his kids. And, like Tony, he had chosen to endure a ridiculously long commute as the price for a "dream" house in the suburbs. Not surprisingly, his health had begun to suffer. Greg started thinking about what was really important to him, and realized that he needed to spend more time with his family. After many long, heart-to-heart talks with his wife, Greg made a double-switch—he took the new job and the family moved into the city so he could be closer to work.

One thing that impressed Greg right away about his new company was how Green Corp.'s senior leaders "walked the talk" by aligning their environmentally responsive practices with the idea of sustainable living. Being green was simply an organic part of the company's approach to support the health, wellness, and productivity of its employees. Although Greg did take a small pay cut by changing jobs, the number of hours he worked dropped dramatically. And yes, he had given up his previous, palatial office. But in truth, he never really needed all that space. And given that no one at Green Corp. actually had an office, the "status value" of a door of one's own suddenly seemed a bit old-fashioned, if not downright silly.

Greg's new workplace was in a repurposed library building just steps away from the subway station. It had plenty of spots where he could sit and work; however, very few seats were actually assigned to specific people. Employees simply sat in the area that suited the work that they were doing that day. For example, Greg often had impromptu meetings with his team in the café area. Management encouraged employees to work at home or remotely any time that they needed to—as long as they coordinated meetings and the delivery of work with their team. This strategy made it possible for the company to reduce the total square feet required in their building, which in turn provided more funds for perks around the office for employees, for investment in productivity-enhancing technology, and for energy-efficient green roofs (roofs made of native plant materials that prevent water run-off and absorb carbon dioxide) and solar panels. The building was a beautiful place to work. After one year at Green Corp., Greg's typical day looked like this:

7:00 a.m.	Wake up, make breakfast, and walk kids to school.
8:15 a.m.	Bike to work and shower.
8:30 a.m.	Sit at the company café and check e-mail.
9:00 a.m.	Write, think, and create new business ideas.
10:00 a.m.	Meet with team in the library lounge to discuss meeting with clients in Singapore.
Noon	Eat lunch with colleagues on the green roof patio.
1:30 p.m.	Check e-mail from patio, using Wi-Fi connection.
2:00 p.m.	Attend high-quality videoconference meeting with clients in Singapore.
3:30 p.m.	Write, think, and create new business ideas.
6:00 p.m.	Bike home and stop by the 'farmers' market on the way.
7:15 p.m.	Eat dinner and read bedtime stories with the kids.
9:00 p.m.	Plan family trip.
10:00 p.m.	Watch the evening news and go to sleep.

When Greg thinks back to his life a year ago, he is struck by how much time he has recovered and how much simpler everyday activities have become. Back then, a conversation with his clients in Singapore would have taken weeks to plan, plus a couple of days in meetings, travel time back and forth, and the resulting brutal jet lag. Now, rather than traveling to visit his clients several times a year as at his old company, he only needed to go to one initial face-to-face meeting. After that, everyone agreed to meet via videoconference. There had been some resistance initially to "going virtual," but this was easily overcome by the resulting benefits. Not only did this high-tech strategy enable Greg's new firm to be competitive in price—minimal travel expenses reduced their fees by 15 percent—it also meant they could meet the project's aggressive schedule *ahead of time* because they were spending less time traveling and more time working.

Greg now has more time to do quality work, to spend with his family, to eat well, to exercise, and to sleep. To the surprise of his doctor, Greg's lifestyle changes seem to have dramatically lowered his blood pressure. Being part of a company with this progressive, forward-looking philosophy has opened Greg's eyes to the possibilities of working in a different way. Still, while he is more optimistic than ever about his own future, he is greatly concerned about his children's future. He realizes that the changes at Green Corp. are good ones, and is glad to be a part of them. Still, he worries that they are only a drop in the bucket of what would be needed to truly begin to repair the damage humankind is doing to the environment.

CLIMATE CHANGE, SWELLING populations, emerging technology, generational differences, financial necessity, and a host of other factors are causing employers and employees to think differently about the nature of work and how, where, and when they are doing it. Tony is so busy he doesn't even realize that alternative ways of working are possible. Although Greg had already made a giant leap forward personally, he is still eager to make a meta-level environmental impact, one big enough to ensure his children's well-being in the future.

There is no roadmap showing the "right" way to work—every employee is in a different situation, with unique personal and professional considerations. But regardless of the circumstances, environmental and economic forces are at play that are unavoidable and that will require employers and employees to change and adapt to a new business environment.

Driving Forces for Change

According to the Brookings Institution, the United States had about 300 billion square feet of built space (commercial, industrial, and residential buildings) in 2000. By 2030, the nation will need about 427 billion square feet of built space to accommodate growth projections. About 50 percent of that 427 billion will have to be constructed between now and then, accommodating both the new space needed and the replacement of existing buildings. Most of the space built between 2000 and 2030 will be residential (over 100 billion square feet). However, the commercial and industrial building sectors will, percentage wise, have the most new space. Brookings projects that in 2030, over 60 percent of the commercial and industrial building stock in the United States will be less than 30 years old. Even if construction is slowed due to economic concerns, there will continue to be a need to support population growth and shifts, and to replace structures lost to fire, natural disasters, demolitions, and other causes. All this development will have a tremendous impact on our cities, our transportation infrastructure, and our lives.

At the same time, federal, state, and local governments are pursuing ambitious targets for reduced greenhouse gas emissions (GHGs) and increased energy efficiency. The impact will be staggering. Executive Order S-3-05 in California, for example, requires a reduction in GHGs to 80 percent below 1990 levels by 2050. This means that Californians will be required to cut emissions to *less than one-sixth* of current levels. At the federal level, the Energy Independence and Security Act of 2007 (EISA 2007) requires all federal buildings to be carbon-neutral—meaning achieving net zero carbon emissions by balancing the amount of carbon released with an equivalent amount sequestered or offset—by 2030.

Demographic shifts also are dramatically impacting the workforce and making the need for organizations to attract top talent greater than ever. According to the Bureau of Labor Statistics, between 2006 and 2016 the amount of workers in the 55-and-older group will grow by 46.7 percent, nearly 5.5 times the growth projected for the overall labor force.[1] When this group retires, this will translate into roughly two workers leaving for every one worker entering the workforce. Many people in the post-boomer demographic that companies will so desperately need to court are very savvy about green issues and increasingly will insist on working for companies that pay attention to environmental issues.

Some of the strongest forces driving change stem from the global financial crisis and instability in the marketplace. Investments and spending decisions that would have gone unquestioned a few years ago are now being held up to an unprecedented level of scrutiny. As a result, companies and employees must make careful spending decisions to minimize the impact on the bottom line and to maximize long-term return on investment.

The pressures to keep pace with growth, anticipate future legislation, recruit from a shrinking labor pool, and spend money wisely during an economic downturn are driving many companies to reevaluate how they do business. Whether or not they have sustainability goals in place, market forces are influencing companies to make radical changes in the way they operate. To compete, they must be extremely careful about how they invest in and manage the assets they have—including their people, their buildings, and their financial investments. In short, even companies that couldn't give a hoot about the environment in the abstract will find that attention to all things green will be critical for the bottom line.

The Workplace Challenge

To meet these formidable challenges, employers and employees must do more than drive hybrids and replace light bulbs. Employers will need to loosen up their expectations about how work happens, and employees will need to radically rethink how they work and live. This means, for example, slowing the pace of building construction, and figuring out how to re-imagine use of current space, rather than chronically replace it. It also means traveling more by train, bus, bike, or carpool—or simply traveling a few steps to one's home office. It also means finding more efficient ways to create energy and transport goods and people to and through our cities. But mostly, employers and employees will have to rethink business as usual. Green buildings can only partially solve today's environmental problems. Companies must change not only the buildings where work takes place, but also the rules related to how people use buildings and what "workplace" even means in an increasingly "virtual-enabled" world.

New Ways of Working

The fact that today's knowledge workers are primed and ready to adopt new models for work makes these changes easier. Many employees already are working during off-hours and in multiple environments, whether it's at home or in a café, car, airplane, or satellite office. Roughly 30 million Americans—one-fifth of the nation's workforce—spend significant hours each month working outside a traditional office.[2] This doesn't even count the far larger number who may not work days at a time from home, but who regularly engage in "flash-telecommuting"—everything from a quick check of the Black-Berry while in the grocery line, to leaving work a bit early and finishing that last e-mail from home. Enabled by communication technology and supported by forward-thinking managers, the idea of "work anywhere" is taking hold. Adopting alternative work strategies (nontraditional work arrangements that affect either work schedule or office location) reduces real estate requirements and lessens the amount of construction and energy and water consumption needed. The requirements for office supplies, furniture, and other operational requirements in the office are proportionately decreased.

Companies see great benefits in alternative work strategies—for recruiting, flexibility, and affecting the bottom line. Sprint Nextel, for example, shed 3.3 million square feet of space from 2005 to 2008 through its smart-growth strategy as well as its "work anywhere" environments.[3] Even if your organization is not ready to engage in alternative work arrangements, it is still possible to reap significant cost reductions and positive environmental effects by paying attention to how much energy, water, raw materials, and land it uses on a regular basis and strategically reducing its use of those natural resources.

Consider the Commute

Adopting new ways of working is not just about saving space, nor is it just about the office itself. Many of the overhead costs and environmental effects of workers come from the act of *getting* to work or facilitating single occupancy vehicle use. One government agency recently estimated the cost of building a new parking structure in its historic building to be roughly $100,000 per space.[4] Even if the organization does not provide parking, annual parking reimbursement can be expensive—up to $9,000 per space in midtown Manhattan.[5] The environmental impacts of transportation, particularly the impact of single occupancy vehicles, are significant. It turns out that the commute to and from work requires more energy than actually occupying office space. Specifically, for the average U.S. commercial office building, transportation energy use to and from that building actually exceeds building energy use by 30 percent. When compared with newer, more energy-efficient buildings, transportation energy use exceeds the building energy use by nearly 140 percent.[6] All of this driving has both an economic and environmental cost.

Smart companies are embracing transportation demand management, a comprehensive approach to encouraging individuals to reduce frequent automobile use outside peak periods and to reduce the distance and duration of their trips.

The Impact of a Green Workplace

Why should organizations green their workplaces? Simply put, where resources are being spent is where opportunities for savings can be found. The most persuasive driver behind green initiatives is that they, more often than not, save organizations money and help enhance profitability. In the words of one banking executive, "If going green doesn't impact the bottom line, what's the point of doing it?"

If you are skeptical, if the concept of green business is new to you, or if for some reason your organization is not yet focused on environmental issues, this next section, and indeed this book as a whole, is for you. It's full of facts and figures that set up the business case for change. As you go through it, and as you plan your own green strategy, keep in mind that companies are motivated by two factors when it comes to addressing the environment: creating value for the organization or mitigating future risk.

Creating Value

Time and time again, companies that have embraced a "green" mandate have created value on a range of fronts. Specifically, they have greatly enhanced their ability to increase market value; recruit and retain top talent;

attract consumers; improve public relations; reduce operational and real-estate costs; and increase productivity.

INCREASED MARKET VALUE

Recent surveys show that companies that address green issues and integrate them into the ways that they do business are improving their performance as compared to those that don't. In 2008, the Economist Intelligence Unit's report, "Doing Good: Business and the Sustainability Challenge," surveyed 1,254 senior business executives to find out how, if at all, stock performance correlated to corporate social responsibility (CSR) performance.[7] The findings include a surprising link between corporate sustainability[8] and strong share price performance. In the survey, companies with the highest share-price growth throughout the past three years (2005 to 2007) paid more attention to sustainability issues, while those with the worst performance tended to pay less attention. A direct correlation is difficult to establish, but in general, high-performing companies put a much greater emphasis on social and environmental considerations at the board level, while the poorly performing firms were far more likely to have no one in charge of sustainability issues.

It would seem that shareholders are more interested in companies that take a longer and more comprehensive view of their business in conjunction with other social and environmental factors. They also are more interested in organizations that are talking about these issues in the boardroom, not just in their marketing brochures. As Alicia Martin, enterprise real estate sustainability manager at Sprint, says, "Our internal and external customers demand a commitment to social responsibility; it is an absolute need for our business."[9]

IMPROVED RECRUITING AND RETENTION

On the recruiting side, much has been studied regarding the "Millennial" generation. This cohort, born between the years 1980 and 2000 (and also referred to as Generation Y), is as large as the baby boomer generation and is just now entering the workforce. They are confident, ambitious, extremely digitally savvy, and conscientious about their communities, locally and globally. One recent study shows that nearly half of young professionals are likely to reject an employer without good corporate social responsibility policies.[10]

Having a green workplace has benefits beyond recruiting new people; it also is an effective strategy for keeping the good people you already have. According to the Society for Human Resource Management (SHRM), 61 percent of human resources professionals polled said their staffs were more likely to stay as a result of their organization's environmental responsibility program.[11]

It matters to consumers

The Carbon Disclosure Project is a nongovernmental organization that works with shareholders and companies to disclose the greenhouse gas emissions of major corporations. In 2008, it published the emissions data for 1,550 of the world's largest businesses. Of the companies that responded, 82 percent said climate change will present commercial opportunities for both existing and new products and services.[12] The market opportunity is particularly relevant in that it strongly appeals to the youngest generation of consumers in the workforce. The 2006 Cone Millennial Cause Study studied nearly 1,800 Millennials. Sixty-nine percent consider a company's social and environmental commitment when deciding where to shop and nearly nine out of ten Millennials studied stated that they are likely or very likely to switch from one brand to another (price and quality being equal) if the second brand is associated with a good cause.[13]

There is tremendous opportunity for organizations willing and able to tap into the green marketplace. Trader Joe's, Aveda, Toyota, Google, Zipcar, American Apparel, and IKEA are some of the many companies specifically using green values to target the Millennial generation.[14] These young consumers are environmentally aware and willing to direct their disposable income toward companies with a green differentiator.

Zipcar, for example, is an hourly car rental service with over 5,500 cars in 28 cities across North America and the United Kingdom. Members of the service reserve their cars online and pick up their vehicles right in their neighborhoods. Millennials are particularly drawn to the fuel-efficient car model options, which include the Mini Cooper, Prius, and Scion. Zipcar claims that each and every one of their cars takes 15 to 20 personally owned vehicles off the road and that, after joining their service, 90 percent of their members drove 5,500 miles or less per year, significantly reducing carbon dioxide emissions. These cars appeal to the Millennials because of their reasonable hourly cost, the lowered minimum age required for rental, and the fact that they are doing the right thing by the environment.

IMPROVED PUBLIC RELATIONS

Burnishing one's image and improving public relations is also a strong motivator for many organizations to integrate social or environmental issues into corporate messages. Take retail giant Wal-Mart, for example. One of the largest corporations in the world, Wal-Mart consumes more electricity annually than any other private user in the United States. Each of its 2,074 supercenters uses an average of 1.5 million kilowatts annually, enough as a group to power all of Namibia. At the turn of the twenty-first century, the amount of waste produced by Wal-Mart's stores was contributing to increased scrutiny—as were their controversial labor policies and perceived "do anything for a lower price" mentality.

In 2004, Wal-Mart CEO Lee Scott began to seek innovative ways to turn the retail mothership from a defensive position toward a proactive and positive direction. Scott engaged Peter Seligmann, a conservationist and co-founder of Conservation International. Together, with an outside team of consultants and the Walton family, the executives embarked on a year-long study of Wal-Mart's global impact. Wal-Mart began exploring everything from agribusiness to organic clothing, looking for ways it could implement its new green strategies while also keeping in line with its philosophy of providing goods at a low cost. With time, continued investment and increased knowledge, Wal-Mart is maturing in its sustainability initiatives, moving toward its goals to use 100 percent renewable energy, create zero waste, and sell products that sustain resources and the environment.[15] In the company's ever continuing battle to enhance its public image, its work on the sustainability front has been by far one of the most powerful weapons.

REDUCED COSTS

In the real estate industry, market demand and a commensurate reduction in sustainable materials costs have reduced the initial financial impact of designing and constructing green buildings. According to a 2007 study by Davis Langdon, there is no significant difference in average construction costs for green buildings compared to nongreen buildings.[16] In addition, the operating costs and market advantages of a green facility significantly increase its value. McGraw-Hill suggests an 8 to 9 percent average decrease in operating costs across the building industry for buildings defined as green.[17]

Interestingly, green facilities not only reduce operating costs, they also increase revenue for building owners, since tenants are more likely to occupy them than nongreen facilities. Building values are expected to increase by 7.5 percent, occupancy by 3.5 percent, rents by 3 percent, and the return on investment 6.6 percent or more for green buildings.[18] This increase means it is less expensive to operate green facilities and easier to lease them, often making them a better overall investment. Corporate real estate executives recognize this fact and are finding ways to green their buildings to reduce the cost of operating them.

Paul Westbrook, sustainable development manager for Texas Instruments (TI), tells how Texas Instruments initially pitched green building strategies within his company. "Most TI employees are engineers by training and logical in their thinking, so they inherently recognized that 'waste is a cost.' Sustainable champions sold senior leadership on reducing waste as a long-term cost-saving strategy. They recognized that, from a business perspective, the cost of waste is an issue, and that if waste is decreased in their buildings and in their production processes, it could result in a competitive advantage for the company. If TI can produce semiconductors with less energy and water, this could be very beneficial to the bottom line." Says Westbrook, "We do this because it makes darn good business sense, and it is good for the planet too."[19]

INCREASED PRODUCTIVITY

Green workplaces typically have consistent features that are particularly prized by employees, including access to views and natural light, thermal comfort, personal control of the environment, and good indoor air quality. These features not only lead to happier employees, but also lead to more productive employees. Air quality research from as early as 1997, for example, estimates that productivity increases from reduced absenteeism and illness in the United States could be as high as $6 billion to $19 billion because of fewer cases of respiratory disease, $1 billion to $4 billion from reduced asthma allergies and $10 billion to $20 billion for decreased symptoms associated with ailments tied to an individual's place of work or residence, referred to as "sick building syndrome."[20]

Mitigating Risk

There are a number of risks associated with *not* addressing environmental issues as part of your organization's business strategy. These risks, identified by Jonathan Lash and Fred Wellington in the *Harvard Business Review,* occur across all industries and in areas that may not initially be obvious. Specific risks include greater exposure to increases in regulations from federal, state, and local governments; threats to the company's supply chain; reputation; the physical risks caused by climate change itself; and increased litigation due to environmental hazards.[21]

REGULATORY

Regulatory risk involves being subject to both current and future regulations. The Energy Policy Act (EPACT) of 2005 and the Energy Independence and Security Act (EISA) of 2007 will continue to dramatically impact business and our economy, with regulation from increased Corporate Average Fuel Economy (CAFE) standards to required energy metering to funding for the increased production of biofuels. The EISA specifically requires zero use of fossil fuel–generated energy in federal buildings by 2030.

According to Don Horn, sustainable design director at the General Services Administration (GSA), this legislation has been a "wake up call." The GSA owns or manages roughly 350 million square feet of space throughout the United States for other federal agencies, and they are not currently organized or trained to fully meet these federally mandated energy targets. To meet them, the GSA will need to make a fundamental shift in its process for designing, renovating, and constructing new buildings.[22]

Significant legislation is not just limited to the federal government. As of March 2009, 935 mayors from 50 U.S. states and the District of Columbia, representing a total population of over 83.5 million residents, have signed up for the U.S. Mayors Climate Protection Agreement. The cities these mayors represent have taken aggressive approaches to regulation and they continue to expand their reach. For example, Boston became the first major city to require green construction for all private buildings that are at least 50,000 square feet in size. What this means for individual companies is that they must stay up to speed with the latest legislation and find partners to ensure they meet local energy, emissions, and other environmental targets.

SUPPLY CHAIN

Supply chain risk applies not only to the product or service being sold, but also the products and services of all of your partners. Using an example from the building industry, a developer may choose an environmentally friendly design, but the materials that are part of the design (steel, glass, and wood) may be subject to environmental regulation, which will drive up construction costs for manufacturers, or in a worst case, even lead to a breakdown in this part of the chain. This, in turn, may affect the project's scope or the timing of the building's construction. Some companies, such as Wal-Mart, have realized this risk and turned it into an advantage. Wal-Mart's Sustainability 360 initiative, a company-wide program, engages and encourages Wal-Mart's associates, suppliers, communities, and customers to place far greater priority on sustainability, thereby increasing the company's positive impact via this "green echo." Given the sheer number of suppliers that partner with Wal-Mart—more than 60,000 companies—the initiative will be far-reaching.[23]

REPUTATION

Companies found guilty of selling or using products, processes, or practices that have not adapted to new environmental standards may face serious marketplace consequences due to a tarnished reputation. In the building industry, facilities that are not environmentally friendly will increasingly find themselves under serious scrutiny from building owners and occupants. This includes buildings that are newly constructed as well as those built long ago. Buildings that do not comply with new green standards face the risk of not being leased or purchased. According to a 2007 Green Building Survey that surveyed 218 corporate users and 166 developers of commercial real estate, 84 percent of corporate users and 77 percent of developers are expecting to own, manage, or lease green properties five years from now, compared to 52 percent of corporate users and 39 percent of developers that currently do so.[24]

Reputation may in fact grow as a factor as time goes on and practices emerge that more effectively measure and communicate a business's "green quotient." In the United Kingdom, for example, a building's energy performance reputation is difficult to hide. The country has just instituted a new energy rating system called the Energy Performance Certificate (EPC) that is now mandatory for all buildings, including residential ones. Every building is banded A through D for its current energy performance as well as its potential energy performance if preventative measures, such as better insulation, are taken. Because this is public information and easily understandable, there are significant incentives for building owners to green their buildings so that they can remain competitive in the marketplace.

PHYSICAL

At a meta-level, physical risk appears to be increasing in tandem with climate change. This can stem from a range of factors, including rising sea levels, increased hurricane activity, crop failure, change in temperature, and reduced water supply. The insurance, agriculture, fisheries, forestry, real estate, and tourism industries are particularly exposed to these effects because of their dependence on the physical environment and the weather. According to a 2007 report from the U.S. General Accounting Office, insurers incurred more than $320 billion in weather-related losses from 1980 through 2005. These losses accounted for 88 percent of all property losses paid by insurers during this period. Weather-related losses have risen significantly from year to year, with claims totaling from a little more than $2 billion in 1987 to more than $75 billion in 2005.[25] Hurricane Katrina alone resulted in $40 billion in insured losses in 2005.[26] Insurance companies have responded to Katrina and other events by restricting those more susceptible to climate change in order to avoid future risk. In addition, they are creating a variety of innovative new products that support the environment, such as green building insurance and renewable energy insurance for wind, solar, geothermal, and similar projects.[27] Granted, these are meta-level issues, and it's tough for a single company to employ a green strategy that forestalls a hurricane. But there is an incentive for companies to pay attention to the physical impacts of climate change and the ripple effect of the damage it causes.

LITIGATION

Companies that do not consider the social and environmental impact of their businesses and their buildings face the possibility of lawsuits. Litigation regarding pollution, environmental protection, carbon dioxide emissions, and mold and other indoor environmental quality issues are increasing. Claims against contractors and design teams also are increasing, particularly with respect to design defects, guarantee of Leadership in Energy and Environmental Design (LEED) certification, and other elements related to green buildings.[28] There is significant potential for workers to file compensation claims for illnesses related to poor indoor environmental quality (IEQ) and class action or personal injury lawsuits due to claims of being harmed from a sick building.

Of litigation regarding IEQ in particular, cases have been related to industrial settings and single-source contaminants such as lead paint or asbestos. According to the Federation of Insurance and Corporate Council (FICC), extensive litigation can result from poor IEQ.[29] When litigation is pursued, defendants include building owners, architects, engineers, contractors, HVAC manufacturers, interior designers, carpet and furniture manufacturers, pesticide applicators, and facility management/maintenance personnel, to name a few. Plaintiffs can be just as varied and include building occupants, tenant companies, owners, and contractors.

Most companies are motivated to fully embrace environmentally friendly practices only after weighing a combination of risks and rewards, and being convinced that there is a net benefit. As time goes on, however, and the rewards and risks alike continue to grow, the greater the chance will be that a fully informed company will inevitably make the decision to also be a green company.

The Future Has Arrived

With a growing interest in the environment from political candidates and leaders, a corresponding spike in media coverage has dramatically increased the "green buzz" around the workplace. Organizations are seeking ways to save financial and environmental resources through a whole host of practices, such as recycling campaigns, work-at-home programs, green procurement strategies, carpooling initiatives, and new building technology. They are beginning to look beyond quick hits and to the full benefits of sustainable actions.

Of course, heightened interest doesn't always mean heightened success of implementation. Green ideas are spreading through organizations like wildfire: in real estate, human resources, communications, legal, information technology (IT), marketing, and in grassroots groups with no formal mission but a passion for making a difference. The difficulty with such a broad spectrum of involvement is not a lack of interest, but the fact that these efforts are not always coordinated or followed through to completion. Truly effective green workplace strategies bring together diverse teams and establish new organizational governance for creative problem-solving. This type of integrated approach can produce "sustainable" strategies that may affect many aspects of the business, including building design and operations, technology use, training programs and recruiting strategies, alternative work strategies, and transportation demand management programs.

And that really is the heart of this book. Not just explaining the "what" of the emerging green revolution, but also the "how" part—what companies and organizations need to do to effectively and profitably take advantage of this new reality. It is not just about the latest green novelty item du jour, but about *sustainable* strategies that benefit employees, the environment, and the bottom line.

Whether your organization is just beginning to think about its green strategy or is well on its way to becoming a socially responsible, environmentally aware global corporate citizen, this book will help guide your thinking about how to move forward most effectively and comprehensively. Environmental strategies and actions that have a long-term impact are about achieving more than high-performing, sustainable buildings: they are about changing the way people live and think about the world. A *green workplace,* in its truest sense, is one that integrates place, human behavior, technology, building operations, design, and business goals. It requires an understanding of green principles and of how people react to change. It requires ongoing research and diligence. Because the green strategies implemented today will almost certainly be refined and improved over time, organizations must be committed to a long-term learning process.

How do you integrate green thinking into your workplace? How have other organizations changed the way they think about themselves and their work? This book will arm you with ideas and examples from many other organizations, ones that faced the same challenges, and blazed a trail for you to follow.

The future has arrived. The question is, will you embrace it, or will you stubbornly fight the tide by lingering in a rapidly vanishing nongreen past?

Chapter 2

The Global Picture

The only society that works today is also one founded on mutual respect, on a recognition that we have a responsibility collectively and individually, to help each other on the basis of each other's equal worth. A selfish society is a contradiction in terms.

—Tony Blair, former Prime Minister of Great Britain

This book examines what it means to have a truly "green" workplace and covers in detail the steps necessary for companies to achieve their green goals. Further, it offers case studies from some of America's most prominent companies and organizations, to demonstrate what has worked for them.

But before diving into all this, one big question looms—why should companies even care about being green in the first place? Is there really a problem, or just a lot of hype? And is the sudden focus on the environment truly something that will be long-lived, or is it simply another temporary fixation, one that will drop off our collective radar as suddenly as it appeared? While it is tempting to write this off as yet another case of "chicken little," doing so would be foolish. The cold, hard truth is that planet Earth—the "workplace" of 6 billion people—is in trouble. And while we may not have yet reached the point of no return, we have reached the point where environmental challenges have begun to have a direct and profound impact on how we do business, and smart companies need to take action.

Our "Supersized" Ecological Footprint

One of the biggest environmental problems facing the world is the ever-increasing depletion of natural resources by humans. This is often referred to as our "ecological footprint," the measure of human demand on the earth's ecosystems. The Earth's population is growing, which in and of itself is growing the collective footprint. Exacerbating the problem, however, is that per capita consumption of resources is increasing at the same time. The net result—a supersized footprint that even Sasquatch couldn't fill. Human development of land and the use of water, energy, and raw materials have increased to a level that is unsustainable. There is more human demand than the Earth has the capacity to regenerate.

According to E. O. Wilson, renowned biologist and theorist:

> The appropriation of productive land—the ecological footprint—is already too large for the planet to sustain, and it's growing larger. A recent study building on this concept estimated that the human population exceeded Earth's capacity around the year 1978. By 2000, it had overshot by 1.4 times that capacity. If 12 percent of all land were now to be set aside to protect the natural environment, as recommended in the 1987 Bruntland Report, Earth's sustainable capacity will have been exceeded still earlier, around 1972. In short, Earth has lost its ability to regenerate—unless global consumption is reduced, or global production is increased, or both.[1]

Not surprisingly, the growth of this footprint has been driven primarily by developed and postindustrial nations, which tend to have a much larger per capita footprint (differences in ecological footprint are illustrated in Figure 2.1). For example, in 2008, the ecological footprint of the United States was 9.4 global hectares[2] per capita; in the United Kingdom it was 5.3. Compare this to China at 2.1; India at 0.9; and Haiti at 0.5.[3] To understand the implications of the situation, it's helpful to disaggregate the overall figure, and look at the use of water, energy, and raw material individually.

Figure 2.1: Differences in ecological footprint.

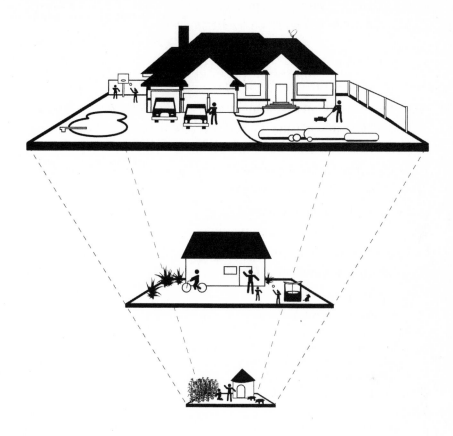

WATER USE

Water is a limited resource. The Earth may look very blue from a distance, but only three percent of the Earth's water is *fresh* water, and most of this fresh water is not available to drink. The majority of it is frozen in glaciers or polar ice caps, or is deep within the earth, beyond our reach. Annual global water consumption has risen almost tenfold since 1900, and many parts of the world are now reaching the limits of their supply. Water shortages occur because of population growth, but also because water is badly managed, spoiled by pollution, or hampered by lack of infrastructure. According to

UNESCO, if nothing is done by 2020, 1.5 billion people will have no access to clean water.[4]

In addition to increased need for fresh water to support a growing population, "embodied" water requirements are increasing. Embodied water is not the water you drink or wash your clothes and dishes with, nor is it the water that flows through your toilet. It is the water used to produce, process, and transport goods you consume. For example, it takes 37 gallons of fresh water to produce one cup of coffee; 713 gallons of water to produce one cotton shirt; and 1,921 gallons of water to produce one pound of beef.[5]

ENERGY USE

World energy consumption continues to increase rapidly, both as a whole and on a *per capita* basis. The United States, for example, increased its per capita energy use by roughly 2 percent from 1990 to 2005. During that same time period, China raised its per capita energy use by 73 percent and India by 30 percent.[6] There are some countries that have reduced their per capita energy use, such as Germany (down 7 percent), but that is uncommon. One of the major drivers behind this growth in energy demand is the increase in wealth of previously impoverished countries. Increased wealth generally means business is doing well in those regions, which means countries are investing more in infrastructure and buildings to support economic growth. Building construction in particular influences the global increase in energy use, given the major impact of buildings on energy consumption. For example, in the United States, buildings account for 39 percent of energy use and 72 percent of electricity consumption.[7]

RAW MATERIAL USE

Raw materials are extracted and converted to commodity materials, then manufactured into products. After use, they are disposed of or returned to the economy through reuse, remanufacturing, or recycling. In the United States, raw material use has risen 5.1 times more than the population during the last century.[8] Think about it: The average American today uses more than five times as much "stuff" as the average American 100 years ago.

Total annual material consumption in the United States rose 57 percent from 1970 to 2000, reaching 6.5 billion metric tons.[9] Buildings are major users of raw material—construction materials, including sand, gravel, and stone—compose the largest component of all raw material consumption.[10] Worldwide, buildings account for 40 percent of material use (and 45 percent in China).[11]

There are other important components of our growing ecological footprint, including the development of pristine land (which takes away habitats from other species) and increases in waste (increasing landfills), but you get the picture—there is a problem.

So what is the solution? How do individuals and companies alleviate or at least reduce this problem? We'll get into that in a lot more detail over the course of the subsequent chapters, but here are a few quick steps to get you started:

- *Minimize water use.* This can be as simple as installing low-flow fixtures in your buildings or as elaborate as designing special features to collect, treat, and reuse water on site. Increase the amount of pervious (permeable) surfaces to retain storm water on site. Reduce the amount of water needed for landscaping by using native plants that don't need watering. When you buy consumer products, seek out companies that have actively worked to reduce the amount of embodied water used to create those products. (Nestlé, for example, has significantly cut water use at its manufacturing plants. From 2001 to 2007, the company reduced the amount of additional water needed to produce 1 liter of bottled water by 33 percent.[12])

- *Minimize energy use.* Lighting, computer technology, heating, and air conditioning are major contributors to energy use, especially in office buildings. Maximize natural light in your home or work facility to minimize the need for electrical lighting, create a more pleasant environment, and reduce heating and cooling requirements. To reduce energy consumption, install building systems that automatically shut off lights, power, heating, air conditioning, and other noncritical energy users when not needed; create policies encouraging employees to turn off computers at the end of the day; and tune up all equipment to keep it running efficiently. Anything plugged into the wall (electronics, equipment, etc.) will continue to use power even when turned off. Green power strips, or devices that stop all power use completely, can help put an end to that.

- *Minimize raw material use.* Buy less paper, less bottled water, fewer paper cups, fewer office supplies, and less packaging, and encourage your vendors to do the same. Encourage employees to use less and reuse products at an individual level as well. This saves purchasing dollars, but also saves time processing materials and paying for waste disposal later. In the proverbial words of German architect Mies van der Rohe, "Less is more." Also, select vendors who incorporate sustainability criteria in their products and services such as using recycled content, purchasing local supplies and labor to produce goods, and taking back products so that they are appropriately recycled or reused.

Our Addiction to Oil

People everywhere are discussing energy, largely due to the recent volatility in the price of oil. U.S. crude oil prices increased by more than 300 percent from 2003 to 2008.[13] And though they later fell, the fear of another spike lingers. But it's not only the price of oil that has many energy companies, politicians, and environmentalists worried, but the "life span" as well. Companies and individuals rely heavily, and almost exclusively, on nonrenewable energy (particularly petroleum, natural gas, and coal). Unfortunately, the global supply of these types of fuels is running out. Peak oil production for the lower 48 states in the United States occurred in 1970, according to the Energy Information Administration (EIA). Several scenarios developed by the EIA predict that global oil production will peak somewhere between 2021 and 2067. Most oil companies are planning for a peak at the earlier end of this spectrum. After this peak, oil companies will continue to be able to harvest oil and gas (including through such means as tar-sands extraction, for example). Nevertheless, there will be less and less of it to harvest, and it will be more difficult and more expensive to find and manufacture into products.[14] For example, crude oil can be pumped out of the ground, whereas tar-sands must be mined and processed to extract the oil-rich bitumen before it's refined into oil, an extremely energy-intensive process.

Renewable energy is generated from resources that are effectively limitless, such as sunlight, wind, rain, tides, and geothermal heat. However, even though renewable energy sources are widely available, they make up only a very small portion of total energy consumption. Renewable energy accounted for only 6.7 percent of all U.S. energy consumption in 2007 and only 0.58 percent of the total energy used in buildings.[15] On a global scale, this type of energy represented only 5 percent of power capacity and 3.4 percent of power generation.[16]

Compounding the problem, the U.S. transportation system is already the largest in the world, and its appetite for non-renewable energy is growing by the year. Transportation is woven into nearly every aspect of life, and is strongly linked to investments in housing, commercial buildings, roads, and airports. Each year, the average American travels the equivalent of one trip around the world. In 2001, 3.7 trillion ton-miles[17] of freight were moved in the United States to facilitate production and consumption.[18]

Ninety-nine percent of the energy that powers transportation in the United States is obtained by burning fossil fuels; 97 percent is derived from petroleum. Public transportation use is increasing, but it's not catching up to our heavy use of cars, trucks, and planes. Since 1970, annual passenger car and light truck[19] travel has more than doubled, increasing at an average rate of 3 percent per year. And U.S. air travel grew faster still, increasing fivefold from 1970 to 2000 at an average annual rate of 5.4 percent. Travel by all modes of public transit has climbed dramatically over the last few years, but, overall, public transportation is still less than 1 percent of total U.S. passenger miles.[20]

So how do we shed our addiction to oil? Sadly, there is no magic bullet, but there is a strong incentive. Those organizations and individuals that find alternative ways to fuel their offices, factories, and homes in the near future will have a competitive advantage over those that wait until oil prices rise above the cost of solar or wind power.

In addition to reducing energy use, something any individual can do, companies that want to take an even more proactive approach can do a number of things:

- *Invest in alternative energy.* If available, use solar, wind, geothermal, or any other renewable energy source instead of energy created from gas or oil. Buy it off the municipal power grid if possible, as this sends a message to utility companies that there is a demand. If your company is willing to make the investment and build renewable fuel sources on-site, look for state or local tax benefits, which can sweeten the pot even further. These benefits may even determine where you invest and will encourage competition between regions competing for your business. Consider investment partners including energy companies. Many organizations buy energy credits to offset their use of nonrenewable fuels or carbon credits to offset their carbon emissions. This may not help the bottom line immediately, but it does help stimulate the renewable energy industry, which can certainly have benefits beyond the short term.
- *Locate next to renewable energy sources.* This may seem extreme, and is not an option for many companies or individuals, but where

Finding State and Local Tax Benefits

Looking for a tax break for your alternative energy investments? To get you started, try a few of these:

- The U.S. Green Building Council's public policy database: www.usgbc.org/PublicPolicy/SearchPublic Policies.aspx?PageID=1776
- Federal incentives: www.energystar.gov/index.cfm?c= products.pr_tax_credits
- State incentives: www.dsireusa.org or www.serconline .org/RenewableEnergyIncentives/greenIndustry RecruitmentIncentives.html
- Your state or municipality's Web site

it makes sense, why not locate your office, factory, or home some-place where there is an abundance of wind, sun, rain, tide, or geot-hermal energy? Google is considering this as a criterion for locating some of their data centers. Choosing a location based on available natural resources is not unlike the way previous generations located their buildings and cities, for example, along rivers or oceans.

- *Reduce driving and flying.* Reduce air travel whenever possible. Do you really need to meet face-to-face? Will a teleconference or video conference call work? Provide policies and incentives for employees to use public transportation, bike, or walk to work rather than using single occupancy vehicles. Use boats and trains to transport goods rather than trucks or airplanes. It may take longer, but the difference in ton-miles per gallon is significant.

Throwing It All Away

The world is using an increasing amount of raw materials and, after these materials are turned into products, the byproducts are thrown away. Though many countries are more likely to produce less waste—Japan, for example, generates roughly half as much waste as the United States per capita[21]—the total amount of trash around the globe is piling up. This is a fundamental challenge of the industrial model versus the natural world, where one ele-ment's waste is another one's food and there is no "garbage" per se.

Waste is produced by all activities related to industry and commerce, with major waste streams including municipal solid waste, construction and demolition waste, and mining, quarrying, and manufacturing waste. Mu-nicipal solid waste (MSW)—what many of us would call "trash" or "garbage"—consists of everyday items such as paper, discarded office sup-plies, product packaging, grass clippings, furniture, clothing, bottles, food scraps, newspapers, appliances, paint, and batteries. Municipal solid waste is the most widespread waste stream, as it is produced by everyone and re-quires major financial and logistical resources to collect, recycle, and arrange final disposal. Construction and demolition and industrial waste generally have a greater tonnage than municipal solid waste, but its management is the responsibility of a relatively small group; that is, those in the construction industry.

The primary environmental challenge with waste is that it is increasing—no surprise given the dramatic increase in raw material use—and large amounts are still going into landfills, which requires a great deal of processing. In 2007, the United States generated about 254 million tons of trash and recycled and composted 85 million tons, equivalent to a 33 percent recycling rate.[22] The Environmental Protection Agency (EPA) estimates that only 20 to 30 percent of U.S. construction and demolition waste is being recycled. This suggests an enormous potential for improvement.[23]

The contents of large portions of the waste stream represent what is left over after extraction and processing of raw materials, manufacturing of products, transportation to markets, use by consumers, and waste management. Virtually every step along this "waste cycle" requires a significant use of nonrenewable resources (energy, water, and land) and affects greenhouse gas emissions.[24]

The strategies for reducing both the cost and the environmental impact of waste is to reduce, reuse, and recycle—in that order of preference. Hopefully you've heard this before.

- *Reduce and reuse.* These strategies have the greatest impact from a cost and energy perspective, primarily because not buying or buying less means fewer materials are purchased or used in the first place, therefore reducing the cost to purchase, process, and remove materials from the point of use. For example, companies can rent less real estate, reduce paper use, and minimize materials required to produce their products. They can also reuse office furniture, lights, appliances, equipment, and so on.
- *Recycle.* Recycling is not as impactful as reducing and reusing materials, but is still more desirable than adding waste directly to landfills. Smart companies have found vendors that will not only recycle their materials but will pay them for what they collect.

These recycled materials are then sold in secondary markets and the company gets a percentage of the profit made by the vendor (or some similar arrangement). You might be surprised about the items around your office that can be recycled and sold for profit, including carpet, ceiling tiles, painted drywall, metal from doors, electrical systems, furniture parts, cardboard, bottles, and cans.

Poor Indoor Air Quality

Americans and occupants of other postindustrial countries spend an enormous amount of time—roughly 90 percent or more—indoors. As a result, the quality of the indoor environment has a significant influence on well-being, productivity, and quality of life.[25] Indoor settings often contain levels of pollutants that may be two to five times higher, and occasionally more than one hundred times higher, than outdoor levels.

Sources of indoor air pollution include, but are not limited to: combustion sources; building materials and furnishings; household cleaning; personal care or hobby products; central heating and cooling systems; and humidification. Indoor air pollution problems have grown in recent years with the prevalence of sealed buildings and minimum outside air ventilation.

Poor indoor air quality in office buildings in particular is typically caused by radon, tobacco smoke, other contaminants, or poor ventilation. In 2002, radon was the second leading cause of lung cancer and is estimated to be responsible for approximately twenty-one thousand U.S. deaths per year.[26] Environmental tobacco smoke, still found in many buildings across the globe, is estimated to be responsible for approximately three thousand lung cancer deaths in nonsmokers each year, and poses significant respiratory health risks to young children, risks that include bronchitis, pneumonia, and asthma.[27] Indoor contaminants such as dust mites, molds, cockroaches, pet dander, and secondhand smoke can trigger asthma attacks.[28] According to a study in 2000, more than twenty million people, including more than six million children, in the United States have asthma. This translates into more than ten million outpatient clinic visits, nearly two million emergency department visits, and nearly 4,500 deaths annually.[29]

How do you keep your workplace squeaky clean and free of all these contaminants?

- *Upgrade furniture and finishes.* If your organization is moving into a new space or planning to refurbish existing space, this is a perfect time to invest in carpet, paint, furniture, and other workplace furniture and finishes with low counts of particulates, gases, or volatile organic compounds (VOCs) that can trigger illness. Select providers with the GreenGuard label that have met stringent third-party tests or the Carpet and Rug Institute Green Label Plus Carpet Program. The California Collaborative for High Performance Schools (CHPS) program also sets a high quality standard for interior materials and finishes.
- *Clean the workplace regularly and well.* Clean work surfaces, carpets, and mechanical ducts according to the building's commissioning plan. Use green cleaning products and equipment such as vacuum cleaners with HEPA filters.[30] Note that you can unintentionally introduce volatile organic compounds into an otherwise healthy environment through a traditional cleaning program. Train cleaning staff on how they should use cleaning equipment and products, such as handling vacuum cleaners with HEPA filters or nontoxic chemical cleaners. Remove or put away all those piles of paper lying around the office—paper collects large amounts of dust, which triggers allergies for the large percentage of employees allergic to dust and dust mites. According to the American College of Allergy, Asthma and Immunology (ACAAI), as many as 10 percent of the general population and 90 percent of people with allergic asthma are sensitive to dust mites.
- *Ventilate well.* There are significant seasonal variations in the volume of air delivered by most heating, ventilation, and air conditioning (HVAC) systems. Ensure that your facility's operators understand the variations in order to provide occupants with adequate outdoor air in all spaces throughout the year. In most HVAC systems, a portion of ventilation air supplied to occupied spaces is

outdoor air and a portion is recirculated air. The total volume of air is important because air movement contributes to thermal comfort. The lack of air movement can create a sensation of hot or stuffy air.

- *Enforce health standards.* Most organizations have incredibly rigorous policies around the use of radon, tobacco smoke, the burning of fuel, and hundreds of other traceable particulates. However, some companies tie their standards to the local government regulations. Many regions have poor or even nonexistent health and safety standards when it comes to these pollutants. If your organization does operate in one of these countries, work toward the implementation of the most stringent standards for air quality and insist that your employees, wherever they live and regardless of the nature of their jobs, have a clean and safe place to work.

    The results of a recent study concluded that reduced respiratory illness, reduced allergies and asthma, reduced sick building syndrome,[31] and increased worker comfort (from changes in thermal comfort, lighting, and improved indoor air quality) would produce an annual U.S. savings or productivity gain of between $43 and $235 billion.[32]

Emissions

Emissions are gases and particles released into the air as byproducts of natural or artificial processes. These byproducts both create greenhouse gases and contribute to poor indoor and outdoor air quality.

GREENHOUSE GAS EMISSIONS

Greenhouse gas emissions come from four main sources, the overwhelming majority of which are related to fossil fuels:

- The burning of fossil fuels to make electricity (33 percent)
- Industrial, commercial, and residential burning of fossil fuels for heat and other emission-producing processes (31 percent)
- The burning of fossil fuels to power transportation (28 percent)

- Emissions produced through agriculture and other miscellaneous activities (8 percent)

In the United States, transportation is second only to electricity generation in terms of the volume and rate of growth of greenhouse gas emissions.[33] Transportation in the United States produces more carbon dioxide emissions each year than any other nation's entire economy, second only to China.[34]

Buildings are a major source of carbon dioxide emissions as well. According to the EIA's Annual Energy Review in 2005, U.S. buildings account for 38 percent of carbon dioxide emissions.[35] This percentage is even greater in urban areas such as New York City, with an estimated 79 percent of total carbon dioxide emissions from buildings.[36]

EMISSIONS AND HUMAN HEALTH

Emissions that impact air quality come from a variety of sources including ozone, carbon monoxide, nitrogen oxides, sulfur dioxide, particulates, volatile organic compounds, and other gases. The levels of emissions that affect air quality vary significantly by country and region. In the United States, even though emissions levels are greater than desired, the rate of overall emissions has slowly decreased each year, both overall and per person. Many developing countries, however, have seen an increase in industry, electricity, and transportation, and the resulting emissions and air quality have become a greater problem than ever.

- *Use less energy, and less energy from fossil fuels.* Buildings, equip-. ment, and vehicles all use energy from fossil fuels, and using this energy releases many of the emissions affecting the ozone and air quality. Beyond the strategies to reduce dependence on fossil fuels already introduced, a few others include: driving hybrids (some hybrids create only 10 percent of the emissions of traditional vehicles); using compact fluorescent or light-emitting diode (LED) bulbs (both are more energy-efficient than incandescent bulbs);

buying durable goods that will last; and buying locally (reducing transportation).

- *Reduce, reuse, recycle.* Buying less, reusing when possible, and recycling are all good options for decreasing the amount of energy (hence emissions) required to manufacture and dispose of materials. As mentioned earlier, this is also a smart strategy for reducing purchasing costs.

The major environmental issues listed here give you only a taste of many of today's complex, interrelated, and weighty environmental problems. The good news is that you and your organization *can* make a difference. The rest of this book is dedicated to sharing hundreds of specific ways to creatively and aggressively solve these problems.

CHAPTER 3

Greening the Organization

There are no passengers on Spaceship Earth. We are all crew.

—Marshall McLuhan, author and media theorist

Employees, customers, partners, and the media expect much more from companies today when it comes to environmentally friendly or "sustainable" practices. A recent study asked over three thousand businesspeople from eighteen countries to rank the social issues that they believed to be most important for global companies to address. Eight priority issues emerged, with climate change consistently at the top of the list. These stakeholders expect companies to lead—not just manage risk—on issues related to the environment.[1] This challenge can be daunting for many organizations that have not made a shift to thinking of sustainability as more than a quaint add-on to what they already do. Truth be told, sustainable thinking that is itself "sustainable" requires major change and transformation inside the organization. The changes must occur throughout, from the actions of individual employees and how they are rewarded, to how the organization measures its success, to how green roles and responsibilities are distributed across the organization.

The Power of the Grassroots

Sustainability has grown rapidly in popularity and, in many organizations, strategies are initiated by employees taking on projects without any mandate. These employees simply believe environmental issues are important and have initiated changes in their personal lives (recycling, biking to work, saving energy) that are transferable to their work life.

Smart organizations recognize the power of grassroots efforts in meeting their environmental goals. These projects are often initiated by very passionate employees willing to spend their own time to make a difference. Engaging these groups is crucial, as they can be one of the most powerful forces for change in the organization. They are the ideal potential champions for firm-wide green initiatives and can help ensure that green strategies are followed through to implementation. If they are ignored or discouraged, they will lose faith in the organization and become disengaged or, worse still, will veer off in a direction that may be counterproductive to the company's goals.

Fortunately, tapping into this passion is easy, since these workers *already are excited* about this. For the most part, the organization simply needs to demonstrate its support and backing and provide these grassroots leaders with the tools they need to educate and engage their peers. Creating firm-sanctioned e-mail lists or intranet sites focused on best green practices is an easy way to both facilitate communication and show support. Further, facilitating in-person localized task forces and groups in which employees can show their creativity can be a particularly powerful motivator.

According to Julie Garden in the United Kingdom, her organization, Cisco, has engaged all levels of the organization in sustainability initiatives. Cisco has a global sustainability board, the Eco Board, consisting of sixteen people, representing each sector of the business. There are sub-teams of the board, which are divided by focus area (Corporate, United States, Europe, Emerging Markets, Asia-Pacific), and then still further, with Green Ambassadors within each region of Europe. Garden says Cisco's UK staff is fully behind green policies and that most initiatives start from the grassroots. For example, all disposable water bottles in Cisco's UK premises were banned in September 2008 (the United Kingdom is the third European country in which Cisco has instituted such a ban). The Green Ambassadors drove this decision—just one of many. Practicing what they preach, even their "meetings" are themselves green. Rather than traveling to get together, they meet over TelePresence (a combination high-quality audio, high-definition video conferencing system). This allows them to share knowledge of what each country is doing, to discuss current and expected legislation, and to decide on new policies for Cisco to take on in each region.[2]

But it doesn't take an organizational structure as sophisticated as Cisco's to get rid of bottled water or to take immediate actions to green your office. One Google employee tells the story of how he took matters into his own hands when he noticed that the "micro kitchens" (break rooms) in Google's Mountain View campus stocked bottled water. He started a petition of employees interested in removing the bottles by using—appropriately enough— a simple Google.doc spreadsheet to collect electronic signatures. Within one week he had collected over two thousand signatures. In Mountain View alone, Google was buying roughly thirteen thousand bottles per day and spending over $1 million annually to stock their shelves. Armed with the petition and a really good business case around cost avoidance, just a few passionate employees were able to stop Google from buying bottled water for all of its North American offices.[3]

Reward Systems

Ask anyone to tell you why going green is important to them and they will likely tell you the story of something deeply personal. It could be a parent who instilled these values in them as a child, the fear that their children need a better world to grow up in, or a vacation they took to a third-world country. You will almost never hear someone say that the reason they value the environment is because their company told them it was a priority. It's important to understand what motivates employees as individuals before you can tap into what motivates them to invest time, money, and energy into changing the way they work and do business.

Wal-Mart understands this very well. The company encourages each of its workers ("associates") to take on "Personal Sustainability Practices" (PSPs) as part of their larger company-wide commitment to sustainability. The PSPs are individual statements of commitment that help associates in-

Are you an employee passionate about the environment and interested in creating your own grassroots movement? Here are some tips to get started:

1. Find out if anyone in your organization feels the same way you do. There is strength in numbers. Some of the best grassroots movements were created by just a few like-minded people pulling together and coming up with creative ideas.

2. Ask your manager how you can get involved. Be forewarned: This is usually the first step to being put on a committee or in a green leadership position.

3. Do research to find out what other companies are doing. Bringing constructive ideas to the table that have proven effective elsewhere increases the likelihood of their being implemented at your company. Why reinvent the wheel? For bonus points, find out what your *competitors* are doing. There's nothing quite like good old-fashioned paranoia that the other guys are getting ahead to help spur even the most change-averse companies to finally get moving.

4. Focus on ways to reduce costs first. Most organizations, if they are not green already, are probably not going to change the way they do business just because it's the right thing for the environment. Costs are important to every organization and you will have more credibility if you bring the most financially viable ideas to the table before anything else.

5. Give your company the benefit of the doubt. Not everybody is as hip to environmental issues as you are. If your company seems slow to act or is "behind the times" in your opinion, resist the temptation to nag or complain. Stay upbeat and excited about the possibilities and focus on what you can affect, which may be just your team. It only takes a spark to create a fire.

corporate principles of sustainable living into their daily lives. Wal-Mart's voluntary program asks associates to improve their overall wellness, as well as the health of the environment. Associates develop their own lifestyle changes—everything from eating organic food to exercising to organizing recycling efforts—that work in their own daily routines and that will best motivate them.

Within months of its initial roll-out, 50 percent of Wal-Mart's 1.3 million associates—many more than expected—had signed up for the project.

According to Act Now,[4] the organization that helped construct the campaign, Wal-Mart and Sam's Club employees have:

- Lost more than 60 tons of weight.
- Walked, biked, or swam more than 380,000 miles.
- Created over 16,000 "Idea Groups" to support one another in achieving PSPs.
- Recycled more than 5 million pounds of aluminum, plastic, and paper.

Wal-Mart realized not only the power of engaging employees and the benefits of this to the company, but also the significant impact their associates could make on the environment and on their own lives outside of work hours.

In contrast, *mandating* change is rarely a recipe for success. Kevin Kampschroer, Acting Director of the Office of Federal High-Performance Green Buildings for the General Services Administration (GSA), has seen his organization live through a number of federally mandated energy and environmental policies over the last few decades. Based on this experience, he is convinced that, ultimately, real changes need to come from individuals and groups within the organization, and not dictated from on high. According to Kampschroer:

> You can try to influence behavior. However, you don't get results by mandating, but by encouraging creativity. An example of this was one of our real estate managers in Kentucky, who was following new standards to reduce energy in his facilities. Rather than just follow the letter of the law, he systematically reviewed the practices of his facility managers and tenants. In one instance, he questioned whether some of the government's 24/7 mission critical facilities truly needed to be air conditioned or heated 100 percent of the time. After talking to the tenants, they all agreed that a six-day-a-week, sixteen-hour day was acceptable for heating and cooling. This simple change affected the government's costs and environmental impact tremendously.[5]

Once employees understand their impact on the environment and the benefits of sustainable thinking in their individual jobs and lives, they are much more likely to appreciate and adopt green initiatives for the organization. And time and time again, it is not the leaders in the ivory tower who come up with the most effective new practices, but rather the workers who are actually on the front line, and have a far better awareness of simple strategies that can make a profound difference.

Measurement

Measurement of the environmental impact of an organization is a difficult and time-consuming effort. Environmental metrics are tricky when we try to tie them to an individual or group, primarily because the environment is open and fluid, and it's not always possible to conclusively link cause and effect. The other difficulty with measuring environmental impact is that there are so many factors at play, including emissions, energy use, water use, material use, waste . . . the list goes on and on. That said, many experts have developed filters for defining the impact of individual or group activities, which are indicative of impact throughout an organization. Companies are beginning to rely on such new business "frameworks" that include sensitivity to environmental issues. Here is a sampling of these frameworks that have received particular attention as of late:

- Triple Bottom Line
- Balanced Scorecard
- Life-Cycle Assessment
- Cradle to Cradle
- Ecological Footprint
- Ecological Economics
- The Natural Step

The Triple Bottom Line (people, profit, planet), a measurement ideology credited to John Elkington in his book *Cannibals with Forks,* is a popular framework used by businesses.[6] The framework is popular because of its simplicity and because measurement of the profit "bottom line" is usually already available. Sprint talks about its workplace strategies and performance using the triple bottom line, which gives a more holistic view of successes. The list below is a sampling of recent success metrics captured by the organization:

PROFIT

- Removal of foam cups provided an annual savings of $135,000.
- Increased volume of recycled materials increased vendor credits back to Sprint.
- Smart strategic planning and mobile work environments rolled out for five thousand employees, resulting in shedding 3.3 million square feet of space from 2005 to 2008. This created an annual savings of $80 million starting in 2009.

PLANET

- Significant savings in carbon footprint and greenhouse gas emissions by reduction in real estate and flexible work policies.
- Reduced paper use by 12 percent in 2006 and 20 percent in 2007.
- Eliminated use of 4.6 million foam cups annually.
- Food waste composting added to kitchen areas.
- Organic pest control for all facilities.
- Hybrid security vehicles adopted in headquarters and regional offices.
- Water recapture system to help minimize water use.
- Low volatile organic compound (VOC) paint used in all construction and upgrades.
- Furniture reused wherever possible, including 90 percent reused furniture in renovated workspaces.
- Low-flow toilets and air hand dryers added in bathrooms.

PEOPLE

- Smart Commute program increased from less than one hundred registrants to nearly one thousand between May and September 2008.
- Corporate Green Team engagement doubled from 2007 to 2008.
- Employees engaged in new Sprint policies and practices with Earth Day.

- Increased employee satisfaction (180 days after moving into a new, mobile space): Ninety-one percent of associates not assigned a permanent workspace were satisfied with their mobile workplace. When asked if they would go back to the way it was before, 100 percent of these employees said no.

Often, successful frameworks for measuring the company's environmental impact are those that are already part of the organization's culture and vocabulary. For example, the Balanced Scorecard, originally developed by Kaplan and Norton at the Harvard Business School, is a very common business tool for setting goals and steering business performance. The Balanced Scorecard model uses the following four organizing quadrants: finance; business process; stakeholders; and human capital, as illustrated in Table 3.1. It can organize environmental metrics as well as other social responsibility goals.

The key to using the Balanced Scorecard is to select measures from each of the four quadrants (financial, human capital, stakeholders, and business process). This structure is particularly effective because it ensures that any green strategies you choose will meet a robust set of criteria. If the organization is choosing measurements in all four quadrants, strategies do not fall victim to the "whim of leadership." Consider, for example, a project or initiative that starts with a leader particularly interested in financial measures. If three months down the road an organizational change occurs, the new leader responsible for the project may be more interested in business performance. But the project stays in play because both leaders see results that are important to them.

Sometimes defining green metrics that make sense for the organization requires creating a unique approach tailored to the organization. Office Depot was one of the first Fortune 500 companies to develop an overall green strategy. This was triggered in early 2002 by the volume of customer requests for environmentally preferable products, particularly paper. By 2004, the company wanted to expand into green practices far beyond paper, including facilities and transportation.

The impetus to better serve its customers, reduce its carbon footprint, and save energy costs helped Office Depot to take another look at energy

Table 3.1   Sustainable Goals in the Balanced Scorecard

Financial	Human Capital
• Income or sales from green products or services • Income or sales from recycled products • Income from waste materials • Investments in green technologies and strategies • Cost of waste disposal • Cost of energy use • Storm water runoff fees • Costs of legal fees or penalties for pollution • Business travel costs • Workers compensation costs • Water and sewer costs • Healthcare costs	• Enhanced personal productivity • Job satisfaction • Percentage of employees using carpools, driving fuel efficient vehicles, biking or telecommuting • Healthy food options for employees • Number of hours of green training • Number of employees with personal performance metrics tied to green goals • Green accreditation and certifications earned • Number of sick days • Number of full-time employees (FTEs) dedicated to sustainable mission • Percentage of employees in green buildings • Increased number of recruits joining organization due to sustainable mission • Increased retention rates
Stakeholders	Business Process
• Number of favorable press mentions due to sustainable or social actions • Number of green awards • Customer satisfaction • Repeat customers • Percentage of local hires • Number of green partnerships • Donations of products or services • Perception of corporate ethics • Publicly stated environmental measures—tracked over time	• Consumption of energy, fresh water, fuel • Amount of emissions released • Percentage of local, reclaimed, recycled, or renewable materials • Percent of fuel-efficient vehicles in fleet • Compliance with environmental laws • Percentage of green contracts and leases • Environmental accounting systems in place • Percentage of green suppliers and partners' performance • Frequency of auditing and commissioning • Duration of use of product or building • Use of eco-efficient products or supplies

savings across its real estate portfolio. At the store level, Office Depot retro-
fitted the lighting to T–5 energy-efficient light bulbs and implemented an
energy management system. Between 2005 and 2006, this resulted in an estimated savings of 66 million kilowatt hours (kWh), a 16.1 percent drop in
total carbon footprint, and a $6.14 million savings in avoided utility costs. In
2008, Office Depot opened its first Leadership in Energy and Environmental Design (LEED) "Gold" certified store in Austin, Texas and simultaneously developed a "Gold" certified store prototype.

In addition to developing green facilities, Office Depot defines its environmental strategy by a committment to increasingly buy green, be green,
and sell green.

- *Buy green:* Office Depot's merchandising teams work with suppliers
  to source more sustainable products. To date, they have diverted forty
  thousand tons of corrugated cardboard from landfills.
- *Be green:* Moving to more fuel-efficient vehicles resulted in a decrease
  of 40 percent in fuel consumption.
- *Sell green:* Office Depot looks for ways to educate the marketplace on
  how to create a green office. These offerings include a Green Book
  catalog as well as a Greener Office Web site (www.officedepot.com/
  yourgreeneroffice). The site gives customers definitions of terms and
  certifications, such as post-consumer recycled content, Forest Stewardship Council (FSC) certification, reduced-chlorine bleach, and
  Greenseal, to help them determine which paper to buy.

Regardless of the measuring system you use for your organization, pick one
that you will be able to work with on a consistent basis. Improvements will
only be seen with time, so switching systems may create issues with incon-
sistent data or lessen your ability to measure your achievements.

New Roles and Responsibilities

Green strategies can be complex and involve organizational, technological,
or operational issues and participation by partners, clients, and vendors. To

say one or two individuals already busy with full-time jobs will be responsible for rolling out a green program across the organization is not realistic, particularly when that organization is a large one. Many multinational organizations, for example, not only dedicate full-time employees to developing and rolling out sustainable strategies, but also see real benefit in adding a position in the C-suite that has accountability and oversight of internal and external green initiatives related to the enterprise. These executives, often referred to as Chief Sustainability Officers (CSOs), typically report directly to the Chief Executive Officer (CEO) and help oversee everything from environmental health and safety, energy, procurement, and regulatory affairs to environmental stewardship, corporate communications, strategic partnerships, and product innovation.[7]

These environmental leaders tend to have disparate backgrounds. Owens Corning found its CSO in research, while Home Depot's Vice President for Environmental Innovation came from its merchandising group. The CSO at DuPont once worked for the U.S. Environmental Protection Agency, while the deputy head of group sustainable development for the HSBC Group came from the World Wildlife Fund. These people are uniquely positioned to make things happen in their organizations because of their access to the C-suite. They are typically respected by their peers and are good with people. Their "likability" is particularly important given the number of people they must influence inside the company and beyond. These CSOs are exploring partnerships with vendors and customers to create green products—and because of their influence and access, they have the power to close the deal. They are also getting a vote—often, the deciding vote—on product research and advertising campaigns.[8]

For smaller organizations, dedicating a full executive position to sustainability may not be possible. However, having leadership on sustainability initiatives come from the top is still extremely important, as it can help establish a vision, set clear targets, and define opportunities.

All that said, to truly infiltrate the organization and create powerful changes, leadership in sustainability must come from throughout the organization. Key players both in administrative functions and within business units must play a role (see Table 3.2 for examples). Many companies have appointed directors or champions to work on initiatives related to each function. Think

Table 3.2   Sample Green Roles and Responsibilities
             Throughout the Organization

Position	Responsibilities
Research and Development	• Minimize water, energy, and materials required to manufacture goods • Consider infrastructure required to support product or service over time • Use biodegradable, recycled or reusable products
Marketing and Sales	• Promote environmentally friendly products and packaging • Use electronic media channels to collect data and sell products and services • Provide rebates or incentives for purchasing in bulk, reusing, or recycling
Operations and Logistics	• Reduce transportation emissions • Minimize packaging, storage, and waste • Incorporate robust repair and recycling programs into operations
Real Estate and Facilities	• Build, maintain, and commission green facilities • Partner with green architects, contractors, and vendors • Invest in smart building systems that minimize energy and water use • Develop a greener waste management plan • Ensure green cleaning and green landscaping practices are used in facilities
Human Resources	• Include socially responsible funds among 401K alternatives • Establish alternative work policies (telework, shared address, hoteling) • Provide green transportation incentives (biking, public transit, alternative fuel vehicles) • Provide employees with access to healthcare (physician, nutritionist, counseling, ergonomics) • Provide healthy food options • Provide opportunities for exercise in or near the office • Train current and new employees in green practices and share green strategies with recruits • Hire sustainability experts
Public Relations and Communications	• Communicate mission, values, and measured results • Develop relationships and channels of communication with stakeholders (employees, partners, community, shareholders, customers, and future recruits) • Use electronic media channels to distribute information (rather than paper)

continues

Table 3.2 (continued)

Information Technology	• Develop green policies for the procurement and disposition of electronics • Train employees to scan documents, use online storage, and order Web-based magazine and newspaper subscriptions • Develop electronic knowledge management systems that reduce paper storage • Train employees to use video and teleconference technology to minimize travel
Procurement	• Establish green procurement policies for consumables, durable goods, and food • Create contracts to ensure partner and vendor compliance with organization's sustainable values
Health and Safety	• Minimize emissions to protect employees and the environment • Provide ergonomic work environment (lighting, seating, work surface, and thermal controls)
Legal and Risk Management	• Consider risks of delivering products and services that negatively impact people or the environment • Invest in renewable energy and environmentally friendly partnerships

about where you might contribute and what additional roles you might take on to do your job in a more environmentally friendly way.

Many organizations establish formal groups that merge some or all of these functions into a Sustainability Task Force or Sustainability Initiative. The more these cross-functional groups can come together the better, as they often inspire each other to take on problems with new and creative green solutions. They are also able to coordinate activities and initiatives outside of mainstream operations. A lack of coordination between these groups is a common mistake and is ultimately costly to the enterprise, as it may result in redundant studies and similar initiatives developing at the same time.

Nortel's CSR team recently created a Green Council that brings together leadership from different corporate groups into a forum. This structure allows for greater focus and clarity and acknowledges the interconnections of divisions across the enterprise as well as the enterprise's impact on the community. It also has allowed sustainability planning to be done in the context of overall business. Workplace solutions include not just space modifications, but also tools that support mobility, such as Internet Protocol Telephony (IPT), laptops, and wireless local area networks (LAN) to enable work on- and off-site. As a result, Nortel has reduced the amount of real estate it requires by approximately half.

Bloomberg's Sustainability Initiative is branded to employees as B-Green. It is designed not only to reduce the company's carbon footprint, but also to educate and motivate employees on actions that they can take to reduce their own environmental impact. This program is separate from Bloomberg's CSR initiatives. The team is appointed by Bloomberg Chairman Peter Grauer and headed by Curtis Ravenel, Head of Global Sustainability Initiatives, and three full-time employees. The team reaches out to the rest of the business through approximately one hundred people from Bloomberg's seventeen operating departments in eleven of Bloomberg's offices.

Bloomberg's sustainability program has a twofold mission. The first part is traditional in the sense that the organization is examining its environmental footprint, beginning with its carbon footprint. This enables Bloomberg to establish a baseline and to set goals to reduce its impact on the environment, realize cost savings, and measure success. Ravenel estimates savings of roughly $8 to 10 million a year in operational costs. Although Bloomberg's business—providing information electronically—has a low environmental impact, the company is committed to the environment and corporate citizenship. Some examples of the actions Bloomberg is taking include:

- *Print room:* Using FSC-certified paper
- *General office use:* Encouraging double-sided printing, turning lights and computers off after use
- *Kitchens and cafeterias:* Providing composting in offices, serving bulk food, discontinuing bottled water
- *Shipping:* Using low-impact shipping methods as the first choice

The second mission of Bloomberg's program is to identify sustainability issues as business opportunities. Bloomberg has added functionality to its

BLOOMBERG PROFESSIONAL service that adds value and fits in with its core objectives. One new feature of the BLOOMBERG PROFESSIONAL service provides information on environmentally progressive, socially responsible, and well-governed companies. Another is a carbon trading platform that provides liquidity to that market.[9]

Partnerships

Your organization may already be involved with researchers, consultants, trade organizations, nongovernmental organizations (NGOs), the government, and the community in some capacity. Which of these partners is aligned with your sustainability goals? What can you provide each other that will create value for both of you? Sandy Thomaes, Senior Consultant from a Canadian financial institution, claims that a significant number of the company's environmental accomplishments have been realized because of its partnerships with architects, carpet manufacturers, waste removal companies, and other vendors. The company specifically seeks out partners that have high environmental standards, and then hires them to help train and implement projects the bank does not have the expertise to implement on its own. For example, Thomaes' company asked some of its greenest partners (HOK, an architectural firm, and Interface, a carpet manufacturer) to help "green" their request for proposals and master services contracts. These companies were happy to help—because they are already green organizations, this gave them an advantage when competing for this company's business.

Partnerships for a green organization can include a whole series of outside stakeholder groups that traditionally have not been partners in the traditional sense of the word. These partners might include a person, group, organization, or system that is affected by an organization's actions that will benefit in some way from a shared investment or joint venture. The benefit of these partnerships is significant for a couple of reasons:

- Problems surrounding sustainability are often so large and so complex that no one organization can solve them alone. Research and development (R&D) costs alone for our best and brightest ideas can be tremendous. For example, General Electric (GE) invested more than $1 billion on cleaner technology R&D for 2007, drawing closer to its pledge to invest $1.5 billion annually on "ecomagination" R&D by 2010.[10] Companies that do not have GE's deep pockets (and even those that do) look to a network of organizations to help them keep track of the latest research and possible green value-add enhancements to their own products and services.

- There is no universally applicable strategy or measurement for moving forward. The good news for the market is that there is lots of opportunity to develop green products or services that redefine the benchmark. The bad news is that there is a great deal of risk involved in picking any one strategy. A multi-pronged approach is probably the right one, and having partners to help you "widen your lens" is critical to maintaining this broader view.

Kevin Kampschroer of the General Services Administration (GSA) describes how his organization has been developing sustainable strategies for decades. Over the last thirty years, the GSA has developed wide and deep partnerships to help maintain its edge when it comes to environmental issues and sustainable strategies. The GSA was the first federal member of the U.S. Green Building Council, a partner with Green Globes (a green-building certification company), and continues relationships with the University of California, Berkeley and Carnegie Mellon. Partnerships with universities have allowed the GSA to have access to more in-depth research than what is typically available from their private industry partners. According to Kampschroer, "We are also helping to push new ideas outwards to other organizations."[11]

In 2005, the GSA sponsored a work session with the Rockefeller Brothers Trust that invited architects, researchers, NGOs, and some of the most respected environmental thinkers to push their thinking even further, develop innovative vision statements, and discuss the latest environmental concepts measurement systems.

Who are your best partners? Well, that's for you to decide. In general, look to ones who have already blazed the trail for you. Find partners that are ahead of you on the sustainability curve and those that will provide you with research, regulatory information, trends, feedback on your organization, or all of the above.

Centralized versus Decentralized Structure

Most organizations agree that some centralization is crucial to ensuring consistent delivery of sustainable activities. That said, in large multinational organizations, there is a limit to the amount of influence a "message from corporate" will have on local behavior, particularly given the importance of regional solutions. Usually, some combination of centralized and decentralized strategies are employed, which vary based on the size and complexity of the business.

The WPP Group, the second largest marketing communications company in the world, employs over one hundred thousand people (including associates) with more than two thousand offices in over one hundred countries distributed among more than one hundred operating companies. Because of the variety of businesses, building types, and locations, the corporate committee responsible for sustainability programs focuses on strategies that have positive environmental impact for their business and are transferable across regions. Many of WPP's operating companies have long been engaged in green thinking—the corporate sustainability committee sees its role as centralizing reporting and building a holistic story around the success of the sustainability program. It was essential for WPP to develop a corporate initiative to share knowledge and to deliver a global green message to stakeholders.

WPP's sustainability program is organized around real estate, technology, procurement, and travel, and the company's approach includes three major steps: measuring, reducing, and offsetting. Policies are adapted and customized depending on the need. In the case of real estate initiatives, different sets of sustainability guidelines have been established for the acquisition of new office space, retrofit of current spaces, and occupancy of existing buildings.

WPP's sustainability program is centralized and closely related to the Corporate Social Responsibility Committee, which includes representatives from different disciplines across the company. This group receives strong support from core management. Having direction and backing from management has been an important reason that the efforts have been accepted by operating companies and executed successfully.[12] Operating companies are ultimately responsible for implementing green strategies and are encouraged to be creative in developing locally relevant solutions.

Balancing responsibilities—and determining what is centralized or decentralized—will be an essential exercise for almost every organization, large or small. The choreography needed to deliver on corporate mandates while encouraging creative, local, and relevant solutions is difficult, particularly when the marketplace continues to raise the bar for environmental excellence. With both top-down and bottom-up structures in place, natural checks and balances occur. Leadership must keep employees moving toward the same target and the people implementing environmental strategies must ensure that those targets are possible to achieve.

Whatever structure makes sense for your organization, ensure that there is a clear chain of command and that all employees are empowered, engaged, and aware of their role in supporting larger green goals. Many employees are confused and frustrated because they do not know who is accountable, and where they can go for the latest information, or what specific actions have been taken by the company. A simple way to alleviate this is to clearly communicate green roles and responsibilities to employees across the organization through internal Web sites, e-mails, bulletin boards, and regular team meetings.

Greening your organization requires a disciplined look at every aspect of the company, from roles and responsibilities to performance metrics and reward systems to engagement strategies to relationships with partners, customers and vendors. Solving environmental problems requires integrated solutions, so organizations must have resources in place to address the challenges that come their way. They also require governance by clear structures put in place to ensure that sustainability objectives are put into effect.

Making Green Stick

Regardless of what is driving your organization's commitment to the environment, two of the most important elements in "making green stick" in the long run are aligning your business agenda with your environmental agenda, and aligning your environmental agenda (at the corporate level) with specific initiatives in the workplace. When these alignments are not in place, they are difficult to connect and may compromise good intentions.

Organizations that are the most effective and convincing to their customers align their business and their green policies by turning their words into actions. There should be no confusion on what success means at the end of the day for all stakeholders. Here are a few examples of organizations that have figured this out:

Toyota Motor Sales

Toyota's slogan is "Moving Forward." The company has made tremendous investments in its hybrid vehicle technology, which has greatly improved its products and services and positioned Toyota as a leader in the hybrid market. As it makes environmental improvements to vehicles, Toyota has updated the plants where these vehicles are produced. The Toyota Earth Charter calls for the company's associates around the world to reduce the environmental impact not only of Toyota products but also of Toyota's buildings and of the overall business. The Toyota South Campus (624,000 square feet outside of Los Angeles, California) demonstrates Toyota's dedication to a sustainable environment. It has one of the largest solar power systems in the United States and exceeds California's Title 24 (the state's energy efficiency standards for residential and nonresidential buildings) by 25 percent.[13]

Whole Foods

The slogan says it all: "Whole Foods, Whole People, Whole Planet." Whole Foods emphasizes the sourcing of products from local farmers through each store's procurement process. This local investment is part of Whole Foods' core business and proves a sustainable strategy from the start. The company recently reached a milestone with its Local Producer Loan Program by administering more than $1 million in low-interest loans to small-scale food producers and growers from twelve states.[14] But the company doesn't stop its social mission with food alone. The company's leadership consistently thinks about its employees and their workplaces, which is demonstrated by the fact that Whole Foods has made *Fortune* magazine's "100 Best Companies To Work For" list for eleven out of the fourteen years that *Fortune* has issued this award. Whole Foods' reduced impact on the environment also has a strong track record. Its stores are constructed using a minimum of virgin raw materials. Its vehicles are being converted to run on biofuels, and the company has purchased renewable wind energy credits equal to 100 percent of its electricity use in all of its stores and facilities. Finally, the company's annual report is referred to as an "Annual Stakeholders Report." Whole Foods' leadership realizes that shareholders are only one of the many groups that have influence in the organization, and the Whole Foods' stakeholder philosophy is the first item on this report:

> Our "bottom line" ultimately depends on our ability to satisfy all of our stakeholders. Our goal is to balance the needs and desires of our customers, team members, shareholders, vendors, communities and the environment while creating value for all. By growing the collective pie, we create larger slices for all of our stakeholders. Our core values reflect this sense of collective fate and are the soul of our company."[15]

Whole Foods' social and environmental goals are integrated with its economic goals, which seems to be a conscious strategy and a major reason for the company's continued success.

Burt's Bees

This company's slogan is also indicative of its business and social values: "Earth Friendly Natural Personal Care for the Greater Good." Burt's Bees has traditionally had a sense of environmental conservation driven by the passion of its employees, and this awareness has evolved into an organized group that is focused on ways to minimize the company's impact on the environment. In 2006, Burt's Bees established an innovative and volunteer work team called ECOBEES (Environmentally Conscious Organization Bringing Environmentally Empowered Solutions). This team aims to pioneer and champion environmentally friendly business practices and to share that knowledge within the company and with its key business stakeholders. And championing green ideas doesn't stop with the products. Within the company, Burt's Bees has long had an aggressive company-wide recycling program and, in 2006, it went a step further and partnered with Sonoco to recycle *all* company waste.

The company also pays half of each employee's cost of achieving carbon neutrality in the employee's household, contributing up to $100 annually.

THESE COMPANIES HAVE tied their basic strengths and core beliefs to an environmental need in a way that increased their value, their brand promise, and their connections to stakeholders. They are successful in their green workplace strategies because those strategies directly relate to the company's culture and employees and customers can quickly understand their relevance and purpose.

Strategies in support of environmental goals are as varied as the organizations they support. As you explore environmentally friendly initiatives for your organization, it is important to keep in mind that not all of them are right or even appropriate for your company. These strategies are not "one size fits all," nor do they fit neatly into a top ten list. They take global issues into account, but to truly work they require a connection to business as well as regional and cultural needs. Here are some questions to consider as you analyze your company's business strategies and how they might tie to environmental strategies:

- What environmental factors are most directly affecting your business today?
- Do the environmental issues your company supports tie to your business goals?
- How can current or future environmental goals create value for your business?
- Does your organizational culture enable or support environmentally friendly actions?
- Is it easy to explain all this to recruits walking through your workplace?

Taking the pulse of your organization upfront will focus efforts moving forward. Also, knowing why you are taking on an environmental goal will help. How many times have you taken on a project and asked yourself, "Why am I working on this project, anyway? Is it really worth it? How does this fit into the big picture?" When it comes to addressing environmental problems, it's easy to get overwhelmed trying to solve everything, rather than focusing on what makes sense for your company.

So now that your organizational structure is in place, how do you get started? What are the right steps to ensure that your strategies are robust and make sense for your organization? The following framework will help you build a strategy that can stand the test of time.

CHAPTER 4

Your Green Road Map

The greatest amount of wasted time is the time not getting started.

—Dawson Trotman, Christian evangelist and author

Creating successful workplaces is about more than just designing beautiful buildings. Architects may tell you that they have designed the perfect workplace—lots of natural light, efficiently organized, and a beautiful place to support different functions—and yet the space may still not work. Why? Because a workplace is more than just a space; it's a complex mix of elements that must be woven together to support work. These elements include good management, communication technology, and training to use the technology. They also include appropriate human resources policies, along with the participation and buy-in of employees. When it comes to a *green* workplace, these same considerations do not go away. Instead, they are just integrated with another set of factors, which include minimizing land, energy, water, and material usage as well as promoting health and wellness in the workplace environment.

Before you read any further, think about why you are reading this book. Is it because your company has committed to building green buildings and you need ideas to get started? Maybe you have just been appointed to a sustainable leadership role in your organization and you are feeling pressure to get up to speed on sustainable practices? Maybe you are an environmentally aware employee looking for ways to encourage your employer to make some green changes around the office? Whatever the reason, consider using the greening of your workplace as a catalyst for greening your entire business.

Historically, when organizational leaders go through the process of defining the requirements for a new or renovated workplace—where it is located, how large it should be, what materials to use, how they would like it to operate, and so on—they must face their core values head-on. The process of improving or right-sizing the workplace requires defining priorities, especially given the sizable investment of money and time. Greening your office may require changing what the workspace looks like, the way it operates, and even the way employees behave in it.

Getting Started

To build a green strategy of any kind (for your building or your business), you must first understand the problems you are trying to solve. Larger environmental issues, such as reducing your ecological footprint, increasing your use of renewable resources, and the like should be integrated into your organization's plan. But there may be other environmental concerns that are particularly important to the company's culture or industry. Once these problems have been carefully identified, it's a matter of defining a green vision and then developing strategies to support these goals.

Greening a single workplace or your organization's entire real-estate portfolio will generally follow five major steps, illustrated as a circular diagram in Figure 4.1. These are:

1. Mobilization (development of a project charter)
2. Diagnosis and discovery
3. Strategy and program development
4. Implications and recommendations
5. Implement, measure, and adjust

Figure 4.1: The five-step process for rolling out a green project or strategy.

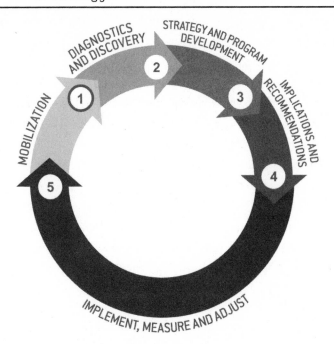

These five steps vary considerably in length and complexity, but each is important for creating strategies that are robust and have staying power.

Step 1: Mobilization

The mobilization step involves organizing a green strategy development team, aligning expectations of leadership and employees, and establishing a project charter. A project charter can be a formal or an informal document that articulates the goals and objectives of the process, the roles and responsibilities of the green strategy development team, expected outcomes of the process, and measures for success.

The best way to start the mobilization stage is with a vision session, or initial work session. In this vision session, bring together key stakeholders to determine common goals and objectives. Because incorporating environmental responsibility into the workplace is a new concept, many organizations will ask consultants or other organizations to brief them on their experiences and lessons learned. Sometimes organizations use a Leadership in Energy and Environmental Design (LEED) or Building Research Establishment Environmental Assessment Method (BREEAM Certification) checklist as a guide, but this list should not be a substitute for defining a vision. The vision should come from leaders and stakeholders in the organization and stem from the values of the organization, assisted by—but not dictated by—a list provided by a third-party sustainability review board, such as the U.S. Green Building Council or Green Globes. Nike's sustainability vision, for example, is woven into their core value proposition:

> We see sustainability as a source of innovation. A way to inspire new thinking and deliver tangible results. We follow a considered design ethos across all Nike footwear, combining premium design and performance innovation with environmental sustainability.
>
> By 2011, all Nike footwear will meet or exceed baseline standards set in our sustainability index. By 2015, we'll include all apparel. By 2020, Nike equipment.
>
> A perfect sustainable product would be one that delivers premium design, maximum performance and zero waste—at every stage of its lifecycle. A dream today, but we believe a real possibility tomorrow.

When beginning to develop green strategies for your business, it is especially important for executives and senior-level managers to engage in the process. One exercise that can set the stage is called the "barometer of change" (see Figure 4.2 for an example). It plots the organization's current and desired state along the continuum of operational, design, and technology strategies. Here is a sample barometer from one work session with the Architect of the Capitol team as part of a master plan for the U.S. Capitol Complex in Washington, D.C. Take a minute to plot on a scale of 0–10 where you think your organization sits today. Would you consider your

Figure 4.2: This "barometer" tool can help measure your company's current and desired green goals.

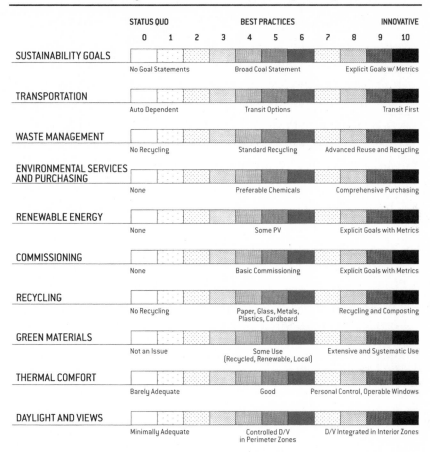

	STATUS QUO				BEST PRACTICES					INNOVATIVE	
	0	1	2	3	4	5	6	7	8	9	10

SUSTAINABILITY GOALS
No Goal Statements — Broad Coal Statement — Explicit Goals w/ Metrics

TRANSPORTATION
Auto Dependent — Transit Options — Transit First

WASTE MANAGEMENT
No Recycling — Standard Recycling — Advanced Reuse and Recycling

ENVIRONMENTAL SERVICES AND PURCHASING
None — Preferable Chemicals — Comprehensive Purchasing

RENEWABLE ENERGY
None — Some PV — Explicit Goals with Metrics

COMMISSIONING
None — Basic Commissioning — Explicit Goals with Metrics

RECYCLING
No Recycling — Paper, Glass, Metals, Plastics, Cardboard — Recycling and Composting

GREEN MATERIALS
Not an Issue — Some Use (Recycled, Renewable, Local) — Extensive and Systematic Use

THERMAL COMFORT
Barely Adequate — Good — Personal Control, Operable Windows

DAYLIGHT AND VIEWS
Minimally Adequate — Controlled D/V in Perimeter Zones — D/V Integrated in Interior Zones

organization white, light gray, dark gray, or black today? What about in the future? Would your colleagues across business units agree? Probing questions that come out of this exercise include:

- What areas are we doing well in and what areas require improvement to meet our sustainable goals?

- How do our current business processes either enable or inhibit the organization from becoming greener?
- Is our business taking a holistic approach to sustainable strategies, or are they residing in just one area of the business?

The answers to these questions should be used to understand not only the current state of the organization, but also the future desires of senior leaders and employees. After the vision session, consider creating a charter or business plan that will clearly define sustainable principles in a larger context. Included in this charter or plan are typically:

- A list of key stakeholders, including internal and external partners
- Background related to the project or initiative
- Anticipated benefits to the organization, employees, and the environment
- Benchmarks from other companies within and outside of the company's industry
- Business need or justification for use of resources
- Criteria for success and measurement
- Risks, challenges, and constraints to achieving goals and measurements
- Schedule for completion, including short- and long-term goals
- Deliverables or briefings to stakeholders
- Communication plan to employees and customers
- Roles and responsibilities of the sustainability team by region and by department

Creating a plan like this takes some work and coordination, but the benefits of creating it are significant. The plan outlines the business case for change, creates alignment and commitment, and defines the resources needed internally and externally to bring the project (or series of projects) to fruition. The level of rigor required to create a document like this will also be required to roll out a successful sustainable strategy in the workplace.

The team charged with meeting sustainability goals may or may not be tied to the organization's existing corporate social responsibility (CSR) structure. This depends on organizational size, industry, and corporate culture. For example, Bloomberg's B-Green Sustainability Initiative is separate from its CSR initiative. Since its program is robust and such a high priority for senior leaders, it addresses a number of unique components including:

- A list of global systemic sustainability trends affecting the business
- Analysis of "business as usual" metrics compared to proposed targets
- Tracking Bloomberg's carbon emissions by operation activity, department, and region
- Utilizing Bloomberg's existing technologies to incorporate green initiatives into operations
- Specific challenges Bloomberg faces with its data centers and customized initiatives for these facilities
- Planning for downstream impacts of green initiatives to help customers minimize environmental impact[1]

If your organization is just getting started, don't let this intimidate you. Start off with a few key initiatives or projects that are meaningful for your company and impact the bottom line. As your program and access to resources grow, you can add on additional components to your plan and continue to set more aggressive metrics over time.

Step 2: Diagnosis and Discovery

After a project charter and direction have been established, it's time to consider where you are starting from. At this point, measure the current state of your organization in order to assess the degree of change necessary. The activities during this phase include making an honest assessment about global and local environmental challenges and determining possible strategies for your organization that can improve the environment, or at the very least mitigate environmental risk. Companies often mistakenly think that their strategies can start and end with building design: "Our buildings are LEED certified, so our company must really be green." A green building is a nice

Figure 4.3: A green business is enabled by sustainable practices in human behavior, operations, technology, and building design.

first step but certainly not a comprehensive strategy, and it may in fact be a small portion of the organization's ecological footprint.

Investigate a mix of building and business strategies that address human behavior, technology, operations, and the design of your buildings, and are each in support of enhancing value or mitigating risk for the business. Adopting strategies from each of these four pillars fully enables a green business (see Figure 4.3).

Green behavior

Modification to existing behavior is the most critical aspect of greening the workplace and the business. Without it, design will be wasted, technology won't be leveraged, facilities will be operated inefficiently, and the business will not capture cost savings or increased value. An obvious example is recycling—organizations can put out the recycling bins, buy the high-tech waste sorting equipment, and post signs around the office that point out the importance of recycling—but if employees do not actually put their waste in the recycling bins, all that effort is for nothing. As another example, an organization might come up with a fantastic carpooling option, but unless employees start sharing rides, the organization will not become any greener. How, then, can your organization influence existing behavior? The primary tools are making a good business case, education, change management activities, a little peer pressure, and ongoing policies and protocols.

GREEN TECHNOLOGY

In the context of a green workplace, technology refers to both smart building technology (automatic light shut-off, solar panels) and technological solutions that enable business efficiency, such as teleconferencing software, social networking tools, or transportation route mapping. Smart building technologies minimize energy and water use and align with existing operating systems and protocols. Technology solutions that enable business efficiency are primarily related to facilitating remote (as opposed to face-to-face) communication, minimizing environmental impact through technology the company has already invested in, and fine-tuning environmental measuring systems.

GREEN OPERATIONS

Green operations are activities related to directing, controlling, and evaluating the operations of facilities to minimize water, energy, and material use. They also include strategies to save resources for the business. Examples of facility-related strategies include commissioning (testing infrastructure to ensure that it is working properly over time), greening maintenance operations to reduce use of harmful chemicals, waste management programs, and training policies to ensure that equipment is operating efficiently. Business-related operational strategies include green procurement (changing purchasing contracts to incorporate green thinking), green shipping and transportation, carpool programs to minimize carbon emissions from single occupancy vehicles, alternative work solutions, and recycling programs.

GREEN DESIGN

Green design transforms the building and physical setting where work oc-curs. It requires minimizing environmental impact while creating a produc-tive workplace for people. It also refers to an approach to creative problem solving, which can be leveraged for all aspects of work.

DURING THIS SECOND step, it is important to clearly understand the current situation of green strategies in the organization. This exercise can either be a high-level or a detailed exercise, but the key is to wrap your arms around attitudes, strategies, and tactics that are already in existence. At a conceptual level, determine basic workplace strategies that have an effect on the envi-ronment. A list of indicative questions that might occur at this stage includes:

- How green the strategy is (overall positive environmental impact)
- The company's current versus desired practice
- Who in the organization should be enrolled to lead and implement the strategy
- Whether strategy aligns with corporate vision and goals
- Relevant environmental measurements (carbon or ecological foot-print)
- Ease of implementation
- Organizational cost (short-term vs. long-term)

The exercise of identifying possible projects is crucial to knowing the ground you will need to cover. In most cases, the initial list of possible projects is very long. Determining their cost, difficulty to implement, and requirements for implementation will be helpful in making hard decisions on what to pri-oritize in the next step. Additional probing questions to identify green strate-gies can be found in Table 4.1.

Step 3: Strategy and Program Development

After defining a list of strategies, plot them out and prioritize which ones are appropriate to tackle first. Though it is often tempting to take on the "low-

Table 4.1   Questions to Ask Before Starting

Category	Questions
Human Capital and Behavior	• Who needs to be involved in developing and implementing a holistic sustainable program? • What about the organization needs to change to establish a credible sustainable program that will maintain integrity? • Are green training programs in place? • Are there incentives/disincentives in place for encouraging sustainable behavior?
Technology	• Are virtual communications available and leveraged? • Do employees store information electronically (as opposed to depending on paper)? • Are smart building systems in place to track and minimize energy and water use?
Operations	• Are policies in place to support alternative work? • Is there a recycle and reuse program in place for furniture, electronics, equipment, phones and other products? • Are green policies in place for purchasing (consumable goods, durable goods, local food)? • Are contracts and leases green? • Are employees encouraged to use alternative transportation?
Design	• Does the workplace provide a productive, healthy work environment? • Are any facilities currently LEED, BREEAM, Energy Star certified (or reviewed by some other third-party)? • Does the building's design minimize the use of energy, water, and raw materials?

hanging fruit" first, projects that are easier to implement might not always have the highest net positive environmental impact. Once the "greener" options have been determined, then you can start with those that are less costly and will take fewer resources to implement.

Let's face it: Most companies do not have a budget for sustainable initiatives and are not always enthusiastic about re-budgeting dollars for a problem that was not on their radar during the budgeting process the year before.

Quick wins that tie to a measurable green impact will enroll management and employees faster and help build momentum. Figure 4.4 is a tool for quickly illustrating how green strategies rank according to their environmental implementation.

Let's assume that you have identified the obstacles to making your workplace green and you are ready to tackle them. Now it's time to create refined strategies and develop a plan for implementation. It's also the time to consider putting some numbers on paper to test the financial impacts of the programs or projects identified. Questions to consider at this stage:

- How important is this program to our sustainable mission?
- Does this program conflict with our overall organizational goals?

Figure 4.4: Compile a list of green strategies and then sort them by ease of implementation and environmental impact.

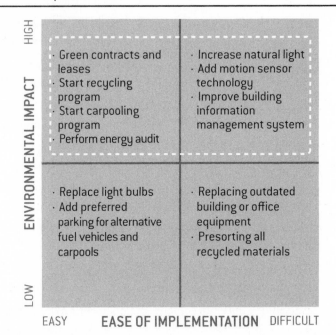

- Will the costs and effort required withstand the scrutiny of our stakeholders?
- Does the organization have the resources to execute this program in a way that will ensure its success?
- Are there other forces at play that could jeopardize our investment in this program today?
- How long will this program take to implement?
- How does each of these individual projects or programs fit into a larger picture?

Each of the strategies recommended should tie back to your charter or business plan. This way, resources spent (even on small projects) can be traced back to larger goals and measures.

Sometimes pulling all of this information together at once can be a challenge. One global financial institution with roughly three hundred thousand employees recently used this process as a means of evaluating its entire real estate portfolio and business practices to develop corporate initiatives. To streamline the process, the company sent out detailed surveys to key stakeholders across thirty business units, then rolled up the results together under seven regions. Engaging many employees in the process (through the survey and other means) allowed the project team to quickly spot sustainable opportunities and challenges across the business. One especially important benefit of collaborating with different groups across the organization was comparing notes about work already done and understanding methodology used to collect or report data across all business units. Moving forward, the company chose to measure its "impact" based on six categories—not just the environment. They considered employees, customers, business process, profit, publicity, and environmental impact to develop priorities and a context for future strategy development.

Step 4: Implications and Recommendations

At this stage, start rolling out project plans and policies that will be the framework for implementation. This will provide the structure for the next stage, implementation. Be able to describe the steps that have happened already and the planned steps moving forward—your green road map. Begin to anticipate the questions that will arise when the "rubber meets the road" and these green programs are in place.

Before rolling out green initiatives at the enterprise level, consider piloting the ideas with smaller groups. Pilots are incredibly useful because they:

- Provide a "proof of concept" and test hypotheses prior to wider deployment
- Provide measures for success that can be tested, with actual results to demonstrate and communicate
- Create support at leadership level for funding because their ideas have already been tested
- Generate a buzz and WOW factor, which will help build employee support

Pilot strategies first, especially if they will eventually lead to a significant change in the organization, and then develop a phased plan for rolling them out at an enterprise level.

The WPP Group has set very aggressive targets to reduce carbon dioxide emissions by 20 percent by 2010. But this will not happen overnight, nor without working through some initial bumps in the road. Meeta Shingne and Andy Hammond, both members of WPP's Energy Action Team, have defined several target metrics to test in three locations in each region: the United States, Europe, and Asia Pacific. They have seen great value in conducting energy consumption audits for selected properties before rolling them out globally. The pilot locations represent not only a breadth of geography, but also a variety of operating companies. For each location, the WPP Energy Action Team worked with the operating company to identify energy management programs that could be implemented with quick wins at minimal or no cost and long-term wins with a good return on investment. The results from these pilot studies will help make a business case for other operating companies across their portfolio.[2]

Through this process, the WPP Energy Action Team encountered a number of issues that needed to be addressed before a full global roll-out.

Often regional differences were particularly challenging. In the Asia Pacific region, for example, WPP's typical lease is three years, which is significantly shorter than the equivalent lease in Europe. This means investments in energy management programs in Asia Pacific are considered carefully, since they require the quick payback. In Europe, larger investments can be made, with the expectation of a longer payback period. In all regions however, WPP works proactively with landlords to understand energy consumption and to share the investment of energy-saving measures when possible.

Occupancy is another varying factor. In the United States, the metric for square foot per person is higher than in Europe and Asia Pacific. Rethinking current space occupancy models (and reducing area per person globally) is a long-term goal that can significantly impact WPP's bottom line and carbon footprint. WPP has established metrics that mandate square footage per person for new construction and renovation projects.

The WPP Energy Action team has recognized the importance of customizing its programs for each region, while still retaining an overall centralized, global strategy, along with an ongoing, collaborative communications program across all companies.

Step 5: Implement, Measure, and Adjust

One of the early misconceptions about adopting sustainable practices is that they stop with the construction of a green workplace or the finishing of a project. In fact, designing a green workplace is only the first step. Ongoing training of employees, facilities staff, maintenance workers, and other contracting staff is crucial to ensuring that the workspace operates and functions as originally intended. But it's not just about reminding current employees or training new employees how to use and operate the spaces they occupy; it's also about improving those practices over time. Our very best green strategies today may be improved tomorrow. With research, and a process of trial and error, new and better green solutions to our problems are created every day. Constant vigilance is required to ensure that these strategies incorporate our most current thinking. This means that organizations must dedicate ongoing resources (people and time) to research, education, and green partnerships.

This last step is where the "greening" of the workplace and the organization really takes place. It's where ideas become reality and change can be measured. It is the truly exciting part of the process and where all early wins should be celebrated. But don't be disappointed when things don't go as planned. As much energy as organizations put into creating the perfect green strategy, there will always be unpredictable events that alter the course. Business happens. A merger or acquisition, staff turnover, or a new green technological breakthrough can wreak havoc with the best-laid plans. Constant vigilance toward metrics and adjustments along the way will ensure that environmentally friendly progress continues to occur.

The Department of Veterans Affairs (VA) has developed a process for greening its workplace that started with a set of guidelines, involved piloting strategies, and is now being rolled out over 1,400 sites and a real estate portfolio valued at over $35 billion. The VA, like all federal agencies, is required to meet strict environmental standards as determined by several federal mandates. In 2007, the VA developed a set of guidelines for its buildings to meet the requirements outlined by the Energy Policy Act of 2005; the Federal Leadership in High Performance and Sustainable Buildings Memorandum of Understanding; the Executive Order 13423, Strengthening Environmental, Energy, and Transportation Management; and the Department of Energy's Interim Final Rule.

The VA's strategies and guidelines, outlined in its "Sustainable Design and Energy Reduction" documents, give an overview of the mandates, an explanation of how the requirements of the mandates are mapped to LEED requirements, and recommendations for adjusting the delivery process to integrate sustainable design, sustainable strategies, cost implications, case studies, tools, and resources.[3]

The green program, developed by the VA and its partners, calls for using an integrated design process, which is not only one of the federal mandates but is also a foundation for achieving sustainable, energy-efficient, high-performing buildings. The organization's green processes require a true collaborative effort among technical disciplines. For the VA, the relationship between technical disciplines was imperative in delivering lower-cost, high-quality sustainable solutions, particularly because of its vast and varied real estate portfolio.

Any sustainable strategies developed by the VA are carefully considered so that they are cost-effective, applicable in all regions of the country, and can be used for all VA project types, including 153 medical centers, 895 ambulatory care/outpatient clinics, 57 regional offices, 135 nursing homes, 47 residential rehab program facilities, 209 veterans centers, and 125 cemeteries. Integrated strategies include those that pertain to the siting of the facility, such as orientation, massing, and storm-water management. Energy efficiency measures include strategies that reduce the overall load within the building, improve the efficiency of systems, and incorporate on-site generation of electricity through the use of renewable resources.

The project team also developed an energy model of a typical VA hospital. The model analyzed the ability of VA hospitals to achieve energy-saving thresholds and examined various energy-efficiency measures that could be included in VA hospital designs to help achieve these thresholds. The energy study complemented the sustainable design manuals, demonstrating how specified techniques could be successfully applied.

Although the VA's strategies were always comprehensive and well planned to start, the VA has continued to update guidelines, strategies, case studies, and tools to accommodate specific project and regional needs and is finding the time and resources to educate its own staff and contractors.

The VA has discovered the importance not only of building a robust strategy, but also of managing and adjusting it on an ongoing basis. After all, going green is a long-term commitment.

The High-Performance Green Workplace

So what do you get after you follow each of these five steps? Ideally, you have a high-performing green workplace that helps employees to be as efficient, effective, and productive as possible with minimal waste and few empty offices or conference rooms. You have a workplace that is full of people communicating effectively, using tools that are intuitive and easy to use either on- or offsite. A high-performance green workplace includes more than just spatial solutions—it incorporates technology, business operations, and changes in human behavior through policy. It provides a variety of "settings" to support individual as well as collaborative tasks. Work is not always 9 to 5—and a high-performance office is on a global schedule that supports work whenever and wherever it happens.

WHAT ARE THE BENEFITS OF A HIGH-PERFORMANCE GREEN WORKPLACE?

- Supports work function
- Creates opportunities for collaboration
- Increases productivity
- Maximizes flexibility
- Encourages learning and knowledge sharing
- Leverages technology
- Optimizes use of real estate
- Attracts and retains top talent
- Fosters innovation
- Promotes overall satisfaction
- Minimizes environmental impact

Beyond benefiting work, high-performance green workplaces create value for the organization. They are productive places that facilitate the kind of interaction and creativity that spawn new business ideas and are accepting of change.

So how does it all come together? Now that your organizational structure is in place, you have developed a robust framework, and outlined a value proposition for your green workplace, it's time to start looking at a wide spectrum of strategies to engage all of the stakeholders affected by your environmentally responsible goals, and get them moving in tandem toward a greener future.

CHAPTER 5

Encouraging Green Behavior

Everyone thinks of changing the world, but no one thinks of changing himself.

—Leo Tolstoy, Russian author

The process of greening the workplace involves changing how organizations construct business operations and policies as well as how they design or redesign their buildings. Many of the strategies necessary for optimizing one's "green-ness" will be described in the chapters ahead. However, even if you bundled all of these structural changes together, the combined effect would pale in comparison with the environmental impact of changing *human* behavior. Green strategies are just as much about changing people's minds and attitudes as they are about greening a building—or even your business. Your office might have purchased the most energy-efficient computers available, but if employees leave them on all night, the projected energy savings is compromised. Or perhaps you have outlined a new strategy to reduce the number of single occupancy commuters to your office. Ideally, this would have a dramatic effect on your organization's carbon footprint and would save the company in parking reimbursement costs. But if your staff can't easily find someone to carpool with, or understand the benefits of taking a shuttle bus or another form of public transportation, alternative transportation strategies will be difficult to implement.

Green Change Management

To change human behavior, it's important to understand the basics of change management. In a broad sense, change management is a structured approach to changing individuals, teams, organizations, and societies, thereby enabling the transition from a current state to a desired future state.

The process of change management is the subject *du jour* for business consultants. And it makes sense. Society is moving into new territory when it comes to change. Employees are being asked to work all over the world and with people they have never met face-to-face. Thomas Friedman's *The World Is Flat* notes that more than four hundred thousand U.S. tax returns were prepared in India in 2005.[1] No doubt, most of these Americans never met their accountant in person.

It's not just the nature of relationships that are changing. Workers are also overwhelmed by the rapidly evolving tools required to do work. Technology changes so quickly that products seem to be out of date before they hit the market. How can organizations possibly expect to roll out enterprise-wide solutions at such a breakneck pace? It's understandable that such continuous shifts are difficult to sustain. The fact that workers are adapting as quickly as they are speaks to the flexibility of the human mind and spirit.

So how does this all tie to the green workplace? It turns out that, when it comes to the office, old habits are particularly hard to break. Even if a workplace is not very pleasant by most standards, many employees will resist changes to it. Transforming an office from its current state to a greener one could involve altering the space, modifying transportation habits, and changing work patterns. Resistance to this transformation will occur at some point; it's not a matter of "if" but of "when."

Effective change management is all about anticipating questions. Think back to when you were a child about to embark on a long drive to a place that you had never been. You probably asked your parents, "Where are we going? Why are we going? How long will it take to get there? Why can't we just stay here?"

Employees ask similar questions when their organizations begin green-ing the workplace: "Why are we doing this and where exactly are we going?" "How long will it take to roll out?" "How will we know if we succeed?" A thoughtful change management plan answers these questions and gives employees a vested interest in doing their part to advance the green workplace strategy.

Benefits of Change Management

Early on, spend time identifying the benefits of addressing human behavior as part of your project. This will help you identify specific ways change management activities can help. In general, a well thought out and well implemented change management program accomplishes the following:

INCREASES VELOCITY OF CHANGE EFFORTS

In just about every project, speed is an important element of delivery. Dragging out initiatives for any reason can create costly delays. These delays, particularly when they are driven by office politics or knee-jerk resistance, are frustrating for everyone involved.

CREATES ALIGNMENT AMONG MANAGEMENT, STAFF, BUSINESS UNITS, AND TEAMS

Given the rate of change in our organizations and the incredible volume of information about the environment available to employees, there is a chance that messages will be mixed and that global, regional, and project goals won't be aligned. A change management and communication plan can help.

MINIMIZES WORK DISRUPTION AND IMPACT ON PRODUCTIVITY

When a project is run well, communication is continuous and multi-pronged. Employees know why they are changing, when they should adopt new behaviors, and how to work through problems.

ENHANCES EMPLOYEE SATISFACTION AND PERFORMANCE

Employees who are directly engaged in the process of changing are more satisfied. Even if they disagree with a decision, if asked their opinion, they are happier in the end.

DISSIPATES RESISTANCE AND ACHIEVES BUY-IN

A healthy change management program seeks out resistance like a heat-seeking missile. Resisters help identify where the problems really are—either the message is wrong or the solution has not been fully worked out.

Green Profiling

Before greening your workplace, consider the different psyches of the people you are trying to change. Not everybody adopts green strategies at the same pace. Understanding the "green profiles" of coworkers will streamline the process. The most common profiles are:

GREENIACS

This portion of the population will say yes to anything when it comes to helping the environment. They are the Ed Begley, Jrs. of the company. They have already purchased their solar backpacks, are using geothermal energy to heat their homes, and have electric cars (or better yet, they bike to work). When it comes to creating a green workplace for this portion of the organization, they are ready to go and are probably impatient for their organization to "get with the program." This group is not afraid to practice what they preach and to share with others what they are personally doing. Organizations like the Nature Conservancy, the Environmental Protection Agency (EPA), and the Natural Resources Defense Council have a large number of employees in this group.

GREEN BOTTOM LINERS

Members of this group are aware of the environment and active in their communities when it comes to green issues. They believe that there are environmental problems that need to be solved. They also understand that good choices for the environment are often good business decisions that can save money and increase long-term organizational value. Ultimately, this is what primarily motivates them (since they are "bottom liners.") This group is already engaged in environmentally friendly behavior. Perhaps they recycle, purchase locally grown foods, or drive a hybrid. Nevertheless, they are not the first adopters of green technology or ideas. They prefer to see them tested before they invest time and energy on something new. A growing number of people fall into this category.

GREEN COUCH POTATOES

This group is willing to try new green behaviors—as long as changes are easy and beneficial to them. They are not interested in going out of their way to try something green, especially if it is disruptive to doing their job. Green strategies that work with this group tend to be low-hanging fruit, or simple changes that reduce costs to the organization. Strategies that affect them personally and make their lives easier also are effective. Examples might be providing recycling bins right at the desk (rather than ten feet away by a shared photocopier) or offering a convenient bus service so that they don't have to walk long distances.

SKEPTICS (AND CLOSET SKEPTICS)

Skeptics are annoyed by the constant media attention given to green issues and believe that, even if there are real concerns about a climate crisis, this is just one of many important priorities. Perhaps they even are champions of one of the other priorities. This group is small and decreasing in number, but must be acknowledged, particularly if they are in positions of influence. Though this group may never enroll in a green strategy, they will need to be considered when targeting realistic green metrics at an organizational level.

Closet Skeptics are people who behave like Green Bottom Liners and give environmental issues lip service, but are not really interested in changing their behavior. They may say they agree with the Green Bottom Liners, but they are just nodding their heads to avoid having to think about the issue.

They have a lot going on in their lives and don't have time for more things on their to-do list.

IT's EASY TO facilitate and build consensus with one of these profile groups individually. The challenge is trying to build consensus with two or more groups at the same time, which is most often the case. Because they are all motivated by and interested in different things, it's important to address their unique points of view. It's also helpful to be aware of the dynamics between them.

During any sort of meetings about sustainability at your office, in your school, in your community, or elsewhere, there is always at least one Greeniac present (what Greeniac would miss an opportunity to talk about their favorite topic?). They are passionate and quick to throw out ideas to push the organization to new levels. The other groups appreciate their enthusiasm, but sometimes feel they are being preached to (especially Green Couch Potatoes and Skeptics). Greeniacs are prone to say "we should" or "you should." Others may react negatively because they cannot relate to zealous environmentalism or dislike having someone else's values thrust upon them. They do, however, appreciate the fact that Greeniacs are like the "mavens" defined in Malcolm Gladwell's *The Tipping Point:* "those who accumulate knowledge."[2] Greeniacs are serious students of the latest green thinking and spend large amounts of time looking for the latest trends, so others believe and trust their research. They are experts in new green technologies and are very aware of companies or countries that have adopted innovative green strategies. This group helps everyone because they have vetted more cutting-edge ideas and practices.

The Green Bottom Liners are a careful bunch. They do not adopt green technologies or behaviors as eagerly as Greeniacs, so Green Couch Potatoes and Skeptics are more willing to be influenced by them. They tend to like strategies that benefit the company *and* the environment. Because of their business focus and healthy skepticism, this group is particularly effective at influencing executives. To them, the whole idea of managing environmental resources wisely just makes good business sense.

Green Couch Potatoes can be influenced, but the proposed new green methods have to be easy and appealing. Also, it takes work to overcome inertia and get them to change their behavior. While they are not likely to be first or even second adopters, if a majority of people in the organization are on board they can usually be convinced. Though this group takes energy to enroll, they often represent a sizable proportion of one's overall workforce and should be engaged. If Green Couch Potatoes see no personal benefit to green behavior, they'll lose interest and move on with business as usual. This loss of momentum can slow or even derail green strategies.

Skeptics should be included in green conversations. Attempting to convince this group to change, however, is probably not worth much effort. In the bigger picture of change management, there is a portion of every organization that will never be convinced. Instead of spending all of your resources working hard to enroll this group, focus your attention on the 70 to 80 percent of people that can be persuaded to adopt green strategies and move on.

Most organizations have a mix of Greeniacs, Green Bottom Liners, Green Couch Potatoes, and Skeptics. People often fall into more than one category or change categories over time. But what really motivates them to change? Is it that their green behavior boosts the profitability of their organization? Is it that it truly reduces their carbon footprint and improves the environment? Consider the benefit of tying strategies to the Triple Bottom Line framework so that they cater to all of these groups and incorporate people, profit, and planet.

People

One common motivating factor among all these groups is the need for green behavior to also benefit them personally. The WIIFM factor (What's In It For Me) is a consistent motivator. Everyone is likely to engage in a green strategy if it saves them time or money. Some groups might be willing to try a green strategy that does not benefit them personally for the short term, but after a while, if it does not prove to be beneficial to them personally they will stop.

Profit

Particularly in a volatile economic climate, saving money (or even better, making money) can be an impactful driver for change. Even still, some groups are naturally more drawn to this idea than others. The Green Bottom Liners are looking to tie green strategies to . . . well, the bottom line. Greeniacs are interested in saving money, but it is not their primary motivator.

PLANET

Money is not the only driver for changing behavior. Greeniacs and Green Bottom Liners are both surprisingly informed groups that are very concerned about the climate crisis. Although Greeniacs may have a longer history of taking environmental action, both groups are likely to consider the environmental impact of their decisions and respond well to strategies that tangibly demonstrate green benefits.

Whatever the mix of people that you are working with, consider taking a multi-pronged approach to influencing green behavior. Table 5.1 provides some examples of ways to appeal to and influence all of these groups using the triple bottom line framework.

SOCIAL INFLUENCE

It's worth mentioning that there are other drivers behind changing human behavior, above and beyond the triple bottom line. Dr. Robert Cialdini, a well-known social psychologist, is an internationally respected expert in the fields of persuasion, compliance, and negotiation. His recent studies have investigated the reasons why individuals take environmentally friendly actions. Among these are saving money and doing the right thing for the environment or society, but he has found that the influence of "social proof" is equally critical to changing human behavior. Social proof, also known as informational social influence, is a psychological phenomenon that occurs in ambiguous or complex situations. When people are unable to determine the appropriate mode of behavior, they assume that those surrounding them possess more knowledge about the situation, so they follow suit. In addition, people are highly influenced by those who are in a similar demographic to themselves.

To demonstrate this, Dr. Cialdini tested this theory at a Holiday Inn in Tempe, Arizona. He worked with the hotel managers to "plant" cards in each

Table 5.1   Selling Green Strategies

Green Strategy	People (Individual or Group Benefit)	Profit (Business Benefit)	Planet (Environmental Benefit)
Work from home	Reduces commuting time and typically provides fewer disruptions Saves stress of commuting and increases time with family	Reduces lease and parking costs, increases productivity of workforce, can be a powerful recruiting and retention tool	Allows business to reduce building footprint and reduces carbon emissions from driving
Use electronic documents instead of paper	Less dust caused by paper (fewer allergy flare-ups) Less cluttered work environment	Reduces cost to buy and store paper and toner Reduces cost to service and power equipment	Saves trees and the energy required to manufacture and transport paper
Use video conferencing instead of travel	Saves stress of travel and increases time with family	Reduces travel costs and increases productivity of workforce	Reduces carbon emissions and hotel occupancy
Increase access to natural light	Increases worker productivity and health Provides a more comfortable work environment	Reduces energy costs Reduces operational costs as it increases light bulb life	Reduces need for power related to artificial lighting Reduces need for cooling space

room with different messages to the occupants about reusing their towel during their stay to help conserve environmental resources. Cards that asked guests to "help save the environment" or to "partner with us to save the environment" got 36 to 38 percent of occupants to recycle their towel. Cards with specific messages that connected the occupants with other visitors to the hotel got a substantially higher number of recyclers at 48 percent. Here is the message they used:

> Join your fellow guests to save the environment. Almost 75% of guests who are asked to participate in our new resource savings program do help by using their towels more than once. You can join your fellow guests to help save the environment by reusing your towels during your stay.[3]

It is important to let senior management, managers, and employees know that there are other similar organizations out there trying these green strategies and seeing real benefits. Sharing stories of these organizations and their success can be just the peer pressure needed to increase the impact of environmentally friendly initiatives.

Identifying Resistance

Change of any sort will be resisted, perhaps even by the most enthusiastic Greeniacs. It's human nature to resist doing something out of our normal routine. Humans are creatures of habit. The key to implementing change is to do the following:

UNDERSTAND THE SOURCE AND LEVEL OF INFLUENCE

Are the people who are resisting green behavior individuals or groups within the organization? What influence do these individuals or groups have? If their influence is strong, perhaps they need to be setting the pace for change—others will only follow.

ACTIVELY IDENTIFY REASONS FOR RESISTANCE

Why are individuals or groups resisting change? Is it because they do not have the skills or ability to adopt a green strategy into their current work process? Or is it because they are not convinced it is worthwhile? Sometimes the solution to resistance is education. Sandy Thomaes, a corporate real estate manager, recounted what happened when her company, a Canadian financial institution, started buying fair trade coffee for its break areas.[4]

Very few people even knew what "fair trade"[5] coffee was, and thus were resistant to the change until an e-mail was sent out to explain the environmental and social benefits. Once employees caught on, they immediately bought in, and many even started buying fair trade coffee at home.

The keys to a successful change management initiative include:

ASSEMBLING THE RIGHT ORGANIZATIONAL STRUCTURE

Green strategies can be very complex and involve space, technology, operational issues, and sometimes partner, client, or vendor participation. To say any one team will be responsible for implementing green strategies throughout the organization is not realistic, given the complex challenges and changes involved. Consider cascading responsibilities throughout the organization through focused task forces. These task forces may become formalized over time.

STARTING WITH A CLEAR VISION AND END STATE

The process of greening the business and the workplace can be overwhelming. It is important to set a clear vision with measurable, achievable goals. A vision sets the stage for change and a clear end state defines measures of success. Many companies publish a corporate social responsibility or corporate sustainability report that provides a public forum for announcing their vision to not only employees but to the full spectrum of individuals and organizations that touch an organization. With a corporate social responsibility or corporate sustainability report, vendors, partners, customers, the community—everyone that does business with your company—will know where you stand. The green goals set for the company will in turn be criteria others must follow to do business with you.

IDENTIFYING AND ADDRESSING THE STAKES

What is the cost of going green? What are the risks of not going green? Play out both scenarios and work through the pros and cons of taking on socially responsible and environmentally friendly strategies.

Developing powerful, holistic strategies and tools

Use robust and comprehensive tools for measuring your environmental impact. There are already several good tools out there. Many in the real estate industry use the Leadership in Energy and Environmental Design (LEED) or Building Research Establishment Environmental Assessment Method (BREEAM) checklist, which are comprehensive ways to measure the environmental impact of buildings. Another tool is the Carbon Disclosure Project survey that measures the carbon emissions of your business as a whole and compares it to that of other companies.[6]

Studying models of past successful change

What have other organizations done to address this issue? What were their measures for success? Did they stick with a plan or deviate from it? Were strategies resisted and, if so, by whom?

Implementing strategy and course correcting as necessary

There is no perfect solution, particularly when it comes to green strategies. In addition, even with the best-laid plans, it's almost impossible to predict the exact course of your implementation plan. It's better to prepare for making changes along the way and to share those with the organization as you go.

Achieving early wins

Find small pilot projects that can be accomplished in a matter of days or weeks. Plan to measure them regularly so that you can prove your success. Here are a few examples:

- Have your information technology (IT) group install a simple "pop-up" message reminding employees to turn off task lights, PCs, and monitors as they shut down
- Post signs in the workplace reminding employees of sustainable practices, such as using only one paper towel, reusing the same coffee mug

all day, discouraging unnecessary printing, and turning off conference room lights when not in use

- Add occupancy sensors to "back of house" light switches
- Switch from bottled water to filtered tap water
- Provide preferred parking for carpools and hybrids
- Install dual-flush valves on toilets (giving users a choice as to how much water is required to flush waste)
- Encourage employees to teleconference, video conference, or web conference rather than traveling to out-of-office meetings

BEING FLEXIBLE

Not everything will go exactly as planned. Besides, society is learning new ways to be greener every day. The targets set now will certainly change and organizations have to be ready to adjust midstream. As Melissa Perlman with Office Depot says, "Green is a journey, not a place. Everyone can always be greener."

Tying Green Behavior to Process

The best processes for greening an organization incorporate changing human behavior along with changing business practices. These activities should occur simultaneously to get the maximum benefit out of green efforts (see Figure 5.1).

DEFINE MESSAGE

When you create a green workplace strategy, you are selling it to the organization. Messages must be credible and use language everyone can understand. Depending on the profile mix of the organization, there may be different approaches for different groups. Solutions need to make sense for everyone. Each green message the organization sends should be tied into larger, enterprise-wide goals. It's important to keep stressing that this isn't just about "doing the right thing" but also about doing the *smart* thing, from an organizational standpoint.

Figure 5.1: Changing human behavior is one of the most difficult hurdles to greening your business. Tie change management practices to every step in the process.

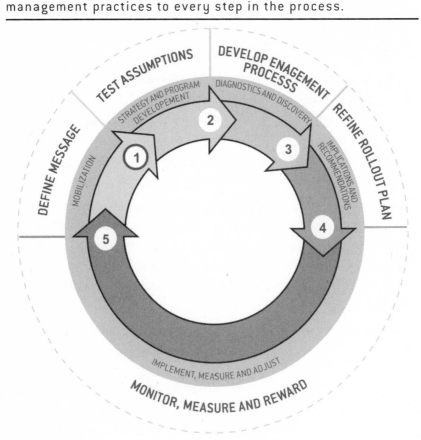

TEST ASSUMPTIONS

Consider the degree of change involved. What exactly needs to change and what are the barriers that will prevent it? Are there systems in place that will inhibit green behavior? How might you remove short-term barriers? Once your green strategy is implemented, who will be impacted, when will they be impacted, and by how much?

It is always a dangerous strategy to use another company's policy without adjusting for unique regional and cultural considerations. Two companies with similar goals may need to implement them in completely different ways because of their organizational structure or culture.

DEVELOP ENGAGEMENT PROCESS

When you're ready to communicate your green strategy to the organization, do it with character, momentum, consistency, creativity, timeliness, impact, and sensitivity to the audience. Be systematic, comprehensive, and holistic in your approach.

Build ownership into the solution. Because many green strategies include decisions that impact the individual and his or her personal choice—alternative work strategies and transportation demand management are two examples—the more involved employees are in setting up those choices, the more likely they will be to adopt them.

So who are you engaging, how are you doing it, and what are you talking to them about? Engagement can take many forms. A green workplace strategy, if holistic, will require involvement from several groups. See Table 5.2 for examples of questions to engage different functions across the organization.

REFINE ROLLOUT PLAN

As a green strategy is rolled out over time, consider the relevance of the message. Because the audience is not ready for details at the beginning, the initial messages should address the broad implications of the issue. Questions that arise at this point tend to focus on why a particular green strategy is important and why it makes sense for the organization's core values. Closer to the implementation time, questions from users will start to become more specific: "How will I need to behave differently in this green environment? Will I be given training so I know what to do?" Just before actual roll-out, the detailed questions surface. These questions typically involve what to do, where, and when.

For example, Cisco provides extensive and regular training for its employees around sustainable issues and strategies. Sales staff are provided with a green video "playbook" for each product they sell, explaining the product as well as its sustainable features. Seventy percent of Cisco's training is now done using these video playbooks. The company also leverages

Table 5.2   Tying Green Strategies to Function

Who to Engage	Questions to Ask
Senior Leadership	How committed are you to this environmental initiative? Would you be willing to sponsor it? Are you willing to dedicate resources to it? What resistance do you see in your organization?
User Groups	Are you currently using green strategies? What green strategies would help the business? What will prevent you from adopting a green strategy? Are there strategies that are easier to implement than others?
Recruits	What are other companies doing? How does this organization compare? What sustainable commitments do you expect and desire from your future employer?
Corporate Communications	How are you currently communicating to internal and external audiences about this organization's green strategy? Is it part of a larger corporate social responsibility strategy?
Real Estate and Facilities	How can green building and workplace strategies support the business? What are the biggest contributors to your buildings' environmental impact? Are building leases green? Are facilities certified by a third party (LEED, Energy Star, BREEAM, Green Globes)? What are the operational challenges involved in greening your buildings?
Human Resources	What green employee benefits are easy to add or relatively low-cost? What policies will HR need to create or adjust to ensure employee expectations are met and that they understand the implications of their green behavior? What sort of resistance to a green workplace strategy will you expect?
Information Technology	What technologies are already available that could improve green behavior in the organization? What green technologies require additional training to be more effective? What new green technologies should be considered?
Partners and Customers	What green strategies do you expect from the organization? What strategies would make you more loyal? What green strategies do you consider best in class?

(continues)

Table 5.2   (continued)

Who to Engage	Questions to Ask
Consultants and Vendors (Developers, Brokers, Architects, Engineers, Cleaning Staff, Food Vendors, Move Managers, etc.)	Are you aware of this organization's green policies? How could the contracts and requests for proposals you see from this company be greener? Do you receive adequate training to know how to better provide green services? What are your most environmentally aware clients doing?

green internal wikis and blogs to share new ideas and trends, and it also brings in scientists and experts to lead training sessions and discussions on climate change with staff.[7]

MONITOR, MEASURE, AND REWARD

Because significant work has been done to develop metrics and measurements around environmental impact, it's fairly easy to share the positive (or negative) effect that green strategies are having on the environment. What is more difficult to measure is the impact these strategies are having on the workforce. The best way to judge this is to ask through methods such as post-occupancy evaluations, focus groups, and blogs. This feedback is crucial for making needed adjustments in the implementation and for giving people a sense of ownership in the process. Testimonials—particularly from people who initially resisted the change—can be very helpful.

For example, HOK's leaders believed it was important to measure the firm's corporate carbon footprint. Doing this required individual participation and engagement. Sustainable Design Director Mary Ann Lazarus, along with several sustainable champions in each of HOK's twenty-seven offices, orchestrated a "Go Barefoot Day" event in which employees were asked to not only measure their current carbon footprint, but also to commit to changing one behavior to positively impact the environment. Employees received prizes for participation in the survey and results from each office were shared with the entire organization. Comparing the current and possible future carbon emissions of each office provided a starting point for change.

Organizations should look for clever ways to reward individuals or groups for their green behavior. Rather than plaques, trophies, or "tchotchkes," consider something a little greener. Here are some fun gifts that fall under the category of socially responsible or green:

- Solar or hand-cranked flashlight, bag, or battery charger
- Green power plugs that minimize power use when electronics are "off"
- Reusable lunch bags
- Gift made to a sustainable cause in the employee's name, such as adopting forests or trees, microloans to third-world countries, or adopting an animal or wildlife refuge
- Subscription to an online magazine
- A day off to volunteer for charity

If the corporate culture absolutely calls for a physical gift, look into more sustainable ways of obtaining the gifts:

- Items purchased from vendors with a commitment to the environment
- Items locally extracted and manufactured
- Items made with recycled content that are easily recyclable
- Items where part of the profits go to sustainable charities

The following are critical ingredients for creating an effective green change management strategy:

Ensure consistent top-level alignment and support

All green strategies must be supported from the top. Although green initiatives often are started at a grassroots level, this does not mean that they stick. Senior leaders must actually lead and support green initiatives. It is also critical to remember that leaders who take on green initiatives are under increased scrutiny. Why? Because their personal choices are scrutinized as much as their professional ones. Employees can be ruthless: they will look at what car you drive, how many houses you own, and even what food you eat. Why? It's not just because employees can be tough on their leaders, it's because greening your organization is only part of the solution—the personal choices you make also play a part.

Make a compelling case for change

Think about the business needs and culture of your organization. What are some realistic catalysts for change? Is it the prospect of creating value for the company? Or is it the risks to the organization if it does not become more environmentally aware? What is the business case that will best resonate with executives, managers, and employees?

Make it personal

Exactly how will your strategies support the individuals who work for you? How will their daily routines be changed? Will their families be affected? Will there be significant benefits that might not be obvious at first? People are naturally motivated by what is in their own best interests.

Try this exercise: Walk through your typical day and the activities you perform that make an environmental impact. Then think through changes that you personally could make tomorrow. It starts with you—your personal actions and commitment to change are the first important steps to greening your team, your office, and your business. Here are a few questions to get you started.

- How do you get to work? Could you walk, cycle, bus, or train to work one or more days per week?
- What do you eat? Are you eating locally grown foods?
- How do you communicate with your coworkers? Do you insist on traveling to see your colleagues and clients face-to-face or are you looking at other virtual means to communicate?

- Do you exercise? Could you integrate exercise into your commute to work?
- What do you do with your waste? Do you recycle at home and at work? In what ways do you try to minimize waste altogether?

UNDERSTAND HOW SIGNIFICANT THE CHANGE WILL BE

What is the scale of change involved? A big change takes more planning, more participation, and more investment from leadership. Changing out light bulbs requires very little engagement with employees—facilities can take this project on and get it done fairly quickly. Rolling out a telecommuting program, on the other hand, takes significantly more coordination with real estate, human resources, security, information technology (IT), and management groups.

ACTIVE PARTICIPATION OF USERS EARLY IN THE PROCESS

If users are involved, especially early on, they will be more likely to adopt the strategy and to feel good about the process, leadership, and the future of their organization. Involvement from employees early on also ensures that strategies have been thought through fully from the start.

Create an enrollment program that ties to specific projects or events occurring in the organization. One U.S. financial institution is building a new 1.4-million-square-foot green office tower. Along with this project, the strategic team is crafting an employee communication plan. This plan includes a Web site that will outline the building's green strategies and technologies—how the building is different from what employees are used to—and will explain how they will be asked to change their behavior.

"We've seen that if people know that specific actions will have environmental benefits, they will alter their behavior," one of their project team members says. "We want them to be conscious of what they can do in this new building."

OPPORTUNITIES TO PLAN AND PRACTICE THE CHANGE IN ADVANCE

Before the organization launches into a whole new way of doing things, practicing and evaluating are extremely helpful. This often takes the form of a pilot group or extended project team willing to try out new ideas and work out the kinks. This minimizes the risk of failure later on. For example, a Canadian financial institution plans to LEED-certify all of its facilities, but has only chosen a handful of facilities to certify for now. They recognize that the process of certification will bring knowledge that will help guide future choices to green their facilities, saving time and money in the long run.[8]

USER DEVELOPMENT OF GROUP PROTOCOLS

Employees involved in the program need to be involved with the rules or protocols supporting a green strategy. Protocols can be as complex as the rules around a Web-based carpooling program or as low-tech as a team agreeing to turn lights off regularly. When employees are involved with these decisions, the result is a culturally sensitive solution and effective "peer pressure" comes into play.

TIMELY PLAYBACK OF RESULTS AND CONCLUSIONS

As soon as results are in, broadcast them and share any positive and negative conclusions. This is especially helpful for facilitating mid-course correction over time. Adobe Systems Incorporated uses an Integrated Building Interface System (IBIS) at its headquarters in San Jose to weave together energy use and other environmental factors in the three towers. Adobe displays this information in its main cafeteria, together with a live feed of energy use in the three towers. Sharing this information drives competition between different tower occupants to limit energy use. "Winners" are promoted via regular e-mails and on the company's intranet.[9]

KEEP THE STAKEHOLDERS INFORMED

Silence is deadly. Once a strategy has been set, continue to update employees on progress. This will minimize rumors, lessen stress over the unknown, and keep the green goals alive. Consider regular newsletters, a blog, an intranet link, or a regular e-mail to staff.

HANG A LANTERN ON THE ISSUE

If an issue comes up along the way, find out what is not working and determine ways to resolve it. Hiding problems only exacerbates employees' worries and frustrates those contributing to the solution.

The biggest thing to remember about changing behavior in your organization is that it starts with you. Adopting green changes in your own life will

---

Change Management at Sprint

Alicia Martin is the Real Estate Sustainability Manager at Sprint. She works with grassroots sustainable volunteer teams in Enterprise Real Estate (ERE) within Sprint's corporate group and throughout the company. She claims overcoming the naysayers—people who think sustainability is a "granola" thing—is a challenge for many large organizations, including Sprint. Making this even more challenging is that the naysayers tend to hold senior positions. Martin addresses their doubts through conversations about how sustainability translates to business success in terms of operational efficiencies and appealing to customers who want to give their business to "green" companies. "This makes it less of a personal issue," she explains.[10]

Martin's change management program includes "brown bag" learning sessions with employees to discuss issues like energy management, recycling, and green technology. Sessions have included mock-ups of green workplaces, discussions about simple changes employees can make in daily operations, and explanations of how Sprint built its corporate headquarters over a decade ago incorporating a variety of sustainability components that continue to grow in number each year. She encourages Sprint associates to submit green ideas and questions through a specific Sprint e-mail address created for this purpose.

Through engagement with employees and strong leadership, Sprint has been able to change the way its people work, not just their workplace environments:

- Sprint has integrated green thinking in the delivery of space, technology, and workplace policies. The company is in the process of moving over five thousand people to mobile "Work Anywhere" environments where they are not assigned to a specific office space.
- Work Anywhere associates (those in the initial pilot program) reported being 30 percent more productive than those in a standard environment—translating to $4.4 million in annual revenue.

give you the knowledge you need to convince others to change. If you take on working from home, or riding the subway, or recycling at home, or buying food with less packaging, you are more likely to understand the changes in your own thinking and behavior required to convince others to change as well. You are also more likely to be listened to by the people you are trying to convince. Walking the talk is important to employees in the organization and paramount to appealing to the top talent you are trying to recruit.

Actions You Can Take Today

1. Measure your own carbon and water footprint. Here's one from the Nature Conservancy: http://www.nature.org/initiatives/climate-change/calculator/
2. Using the results, pick three things in your own life you can do to reduce your carbon or water footprint and take action.
3. Reward yourself for green behavior. Buy a new bicycle with that money you saved on your electric bill.
4. Profile yourself and your team. Is your group full of Green Bottom Liners or Green Couch Potatoes? Is your group reflective of the culture of the organization? If so, what are the major cultural hurdles you expect to face?
5. What green strategies can your organization take on today and implement in weeks, not months?
6. How will you measure success? Is it a reduction in carbon footprint, a reduction of energy use, or a percentage engagement of a population?
7. Read a green blog, magazine, or book that interests you, or take a class if you learn better that way. Environmental issues are complex and require some education to fully comprehend. If you are trying to convince others to change, you'll need some ammunition. Try some of these books to start:

   - *Ecology of Commerce: A Declaration of Sustainability*, Paul Hawken
   - *Green to Gold: How Smart Companies Use Environmental Strategies to Innovate, Create Value, and Build Competitive Advantage*, Daniel C. Esty and Andrew S. Winston
   - *Mid-Course Correction: Toward a Sustainable Enterprise: The Interface Model*, Ray Anderson
   - *Cradle to Cradle: Remaking the Way We Make Things*, William McDonough and Michael Braungart

CHAPTER 6

Green Recruiting

I think the younger generation, the people poised to dominate the work-force, is more socially conscious. They are more demanding in terms of [the] environment and how that environment contributes to their life.

—Helmut Jahn, German-American architect

If your company is looking to recruit and retain bright, motivated employees, chances are you'll have to offer more than a good salary to win them over. To attract and retain high-caliber people, companies need to connect with employees on multiple levels. When hiring top talent—particularly younger talent—a company's approach to sustainability and the environment can either be a powerful lure for wooing such talent, or the unintended repellent that pushes them somewhere else.

Green recruiting offers an opportunity to differentiate your organization. Organizations that use socially aware and environmentally friendly strategies to recruit and retain employees understand that:

- The youngest generation in the workforce, the Millennials, grew up with a heightened environmental awareness and are now actively seeking green employment opportunities.[1]

- Recent college graduates have embraced sustainable principles and believe that every aspect of their lives, including their job, should leave a minimal environmental footprint.[2]

But it's not just younger applicants who can be netted through green recruiting. Many job candidates of all ages simply have a preference for green jobs. In a report from The Center for Corporate Citizenship and Sustainability, 78 percent of the 198 multinational companies surveyed described corporate citizenship (including sustainable practices) as very or extremely important in attracting and retaining employees.[3] In an Adecco poll, 33 percent of the 2,500 U.S. adults surveyed replied that they would be more inclined to work for a green company.[4] It's not that a company's environmental policy is the only factor in a potential employee's choice. But, all things being equal, this is a big differentiator.

The Society for Human Resource Management (SHRM) surveyed human resources professionals and employees to determine attitudes toward sustainability in the workplace. The survey found that many employees see the benefits of sustainable practices, listing the two top outcomes of sustainable behavior in an organization as improved employee morale and stronger public image.[5] Additionally, as Charlotte Huff pointed out in an article in *Workforce Management,* environmental sensitivity is one shorthand way to assess how a company treats its employees: "It shows that this company cares for something more than just profits."[6]

Sustainability and other corporate social responsibility (CSR) initiatives can be attractive to potential employees. However, many recruits check the background of organizations and talk with employees or past employees to determine whether green or CSR messaging is legitimate or if it is "greenwashing." As Gerlinde Herrmann points out: "Better to have genuine green or CSR initiatives which are grassroots and inexpensive than to have a massive promotional campaign involving significant funding—it's the realness that is the selling feature."[7]

Green recruiting is about using the company's green practices to attract and retain employees; however, it must be done in a way that is sustainable as well. To implement a green recruiting strategy, companies should consider a multi-pronged approach: incorporating sustainability into branding

Greenwashing

"Greenwashing" is a term, first used in the 1990s, that refers to the act of misleading others regarding the environmental practices of a company or the environmental benefits of a product or service. For example, a bottle of toxic cleaning chemicals may have an image of lakes and forests on the front to give the impression that it is good for the environment. Or a product may be listed as "certified" green, but doesn't say who certified it. TerraChoice, an environmental marketing agency, released a study in December 2007: "The Six Sins of Greenwashing."[8] These include:

1. Suggesting that a product or practice is "green" based on a single aspect of production without acknowledging nongreen aspects.
2. A claim that cannot be substantiated or has no third-party certification from a reliable source.
3. A claim that is so broad or vague that the real meaning is hidden or misunderstood.
4. A claim that may be truthful, but bears no relevance.
5. Outright lying about the green aspects of the product or service.
6. Claims that may be true, but risk distracting the consumer from the greater environmental impacts, such as "organic cigarettes."

While greenwashing can be tempting (and even may occur accidentally), the rise of corporate social responsibility puts pressure on organizations to become smarter and more open about how their products and services are delivered.

and corporate culture; finding green-friendly venues for recruiting; offering green job descriptions; providing green benefits; and greening the recruiting process itself.

Green Branding and Organizational Culture

One of the best ways to prove to potential recruits your organization's commitment to sustainability is to practice what you preach. This involves not only instilling green values and practices, but also promoting them. By making green part of the company's brand, and by making sure that it's based on a solid foundation of reality, the organizational commitment to the environment becomes more visible and credible to existing employees and recruits and can increase the attractiveness of working for the company.

When it comes to branding, environmental messages fit into one of two categories: applied or integrated. Applied branding is the full-color images you see on Web sites and in corporate recruiting and marketing materials. It's very nice-looking, and tells a good story, but is not always convincing to a skeptical recruit. Integrated branding refers to the corporate culture, and speaks to how every activity in the organization reinforces key messages that reflect a strong environmental commitment. For example, take recycling. Some organizations put out public statements about their commitment to reducing waste and recycling—this is applied branding. But if an office has recycling bins everywhere or compost bins in kitchenettes, this is an example of integrated branding. And integrated branding is far more compelling to someone looking to work for a green company.

Many organizations have always been committed to making green strategies part of their integrated brand. The BMW Group is a great example. This German-owned organization has always been passionate about the environment—a fact that is reflected in its culture as well as in the lifelong values of investors in the company. As early as the 1970s, BMW introduced an electric powered car and was the first car manufacturer to appoint an environmental officer.[9] Less environmentally savvy companies, however, are having to work hard to play catch-up, and to transform themselves and their employees into a more socially and environmentally aware community.

In order to instill environmentally responsible thinking in your corporate culture and brand, your organization must first develop and implement clear environmental policies that promote an eco-healthy workplace and lifestyle. Once these are in place, it is much easier to credibly publicize the company's environmental record and approach. Many companies choose to list sustainable measures in their annual report, while others prepare a separate corporate social responsibility report with facts and figures related to sustainable initiatives. These reports do more than highlight environmental accolades or awards and show pictures of native forests; they focus on green initiatives taken by the company and its employees on a day-to-day basis in the workplace. These might include a statement of policies or statistics on a program's success, such as the number of pounds of recycling or the amount of money or paper saved as a result of e-filing. Employee and client testimonials also send a powerful message to potential recruits and customers.

In addition to exposing the company's commitment to greening internal operations, companies that get positive media attention take socially and environmentally beneficial actions that go beyond their organization. Successful companies make use of these opportunities to increase awareness of their sustainable initiatives and promote their beliefs. The more creative their efforts, and the more they emphasize the message of practicing environmentally friendly thinking, the more likely they are to attract attention from recruits, stakeholders, and customers. Some great examples of this include:

GOOGLE'S SOLAR INVESTMENTS

In 2006, Google announced that it would be converting its headquarters to run partly on solar energy via one of the largest corporate solar installations in the United States. This gave the company lots of positive media buzz, but also was a wise business move. The sun now delivers 30 percent of the electricity needed to power the Google buildings on which panels are located.[10]

DELL'S GREEN WORKPLACE MAKEOVER

As part of the launch for a green product line, Dell gave a "green workplace makeover" to one of its small-business customers, Robertson Homes, in St. Cloud, Florida. Dell donated new energy-efficient monitors, computers, and servers to Robertson Homes and hired specialists to help this company look at other forms of energy savings around the office. Dell caught it all on film to share with other small businesses on its external blog. By doing this, Dell helped one of its clients save energy and also invested in local green-collar jobs by helping this small green company (Robertson Homes builds energy efficient housing).[11] And, of course, Dell also just happened to get a lot of nice buzz in the process.

PROGRESSIVE AUTOMOTIVE X PRIZE

Progressive Insurance, a company with a long history of CSR involvement, is sponsoring a competition for those who can engineer clean, production-capable vehicles that exceed a fuel efficiency of 100 miles per gallon. The prize—$10 million—sends a clear signal as to Progressive's commitment to energy efficiency.[12]

IN EACH OF these examples, the company may or may not have reaped some direct financial benefits, but there is no doubt that they benefited greatly from the "brand halo" effect of demonstrating such a strong commitment to the environment.

Recruiting Venues

While it may be easy to find entry-level candidates interested in sustainability (most college campuses are hotbeds of environmentalists), more experienced environmentally focused employees are still not as easy to find. And chances are, they're not showing up at your doorstep in droves. Thus, in order to attract the most green-savvy employees for your company, you may need to turn to outside sources.

One of the most effective ways to find these candidates is through word-of-mouth. Any time employees are at green events or trade shows, it is an opportunity to find candidates with similar interests. Other options for recruiting include:

- Networking with environmentally friendly organizations, such as the Sierra Club, the U.S. Green Building Council, or local environment groups or non-profits
- Using recruiters or head hunters who are committed to environmental causes
- "Renting" e-mail lists from environmentally friendly publications, i.e., paying for the right to have them send a message for you
- Using online job sites that focus on green jobs, such as Monster.com's GreenCareers, Idealist.org, GreenJobSearch.com, SustainableBusiness.com, and GreenBiz.com

Job Descriptions

In recent years, there has been talk about "green-collar" jobs—typically referring to one of two types of employment:

HOK's Recruiting Strategies

As an architecture firm that has long embraced sustainable design, HOK is always on the lookout for candidates with an interest in the environment. Today, students are becoming smarter about the questions they ask and they watch for companies that are practicing what they preach.

One recruiting strategy that HOK now uses is that all candidates must apply through an online resume database. This system has been in place since 2001 and, because of it, the number of unsolicited paper resumes has gone down by at least 75 percent.

In addition, HOK has launched several recruiting campaigns online through its "Life at HOK" blog (www.hoklife.com) and through corporate pages on Facebook, LinkedIn, Flickr, Twitter, and other social networking sites. This has not only increased the frequency and value of interaction with recruits, but has also reduced face-to-face recruiting travel, not to mention dramatically reducing the amount of paper recruiting materials needed.

- Local positions that are focused on keeping dollars spent within smaller regional communities to boost local growth and minimize environmental impact
- Jobs that are tied to renewable energy and energy efficiency sectors

Just because a job does not fall into one of these "green-collar" categories does not mean it cannot or should not have environmental responsibilities. Every job can be a green-collar job in the sense that every employee, from the receptionist to the Corporate Sustainability Officer, can have green responsibilities. Everyone can contribute to using less paper, turning off their computers at night, turning off lights when a room is not occupied, recycling materials, and just doing one's job with a sensitivity to saving resources whenever possible. Corporate policies can be attached to job descriptions, which will send a strong message of commitment.

To attract new employees with an affinity for green, it is important to provide job descriptions that not only depict the traditional responsibilities of the position but also include responsibilities for minimizing environmental impact. An additional way to attract future employees who are serious about the environment is to include a request for knowledge or experience about environmental issues that relate to the job duties of the advertised position. This could range from past experience to training to professional accreditation. Finding candidates through traditional channels (such as advertised job descriptions) isn't the only way to seek out bright, environmentally savvy people. Some recruiters claim they've even found qualified candidates by reading what candidates have written on green or environmentally focused blogs.

Green Benefits

Candidates with a commitment to sustainability and environmentalism will expect employers to promote sustainability throughout their business practice. One way to demonstrate this is to offer green benefits as part of the compensation package: benefits that are good for both the employee and the environment.

Green benefits might come either directly through compensation or through the workplace practices. Some examples of compensation benefits include:

- Socially responsible funds in the 401K package
- Donations to a green cause in an employee's name
- Subsidies for hybrid or other alternative fuel automobiles
- Subsidies for alternative transportation methods, such as subway or bus
- Free sustainable learning events or training sessions, or reimbursement for attending third-party sessions

Many companies have realized the value in providing other "green services" in the workplace or, when this is not possible, offering benefits that enable employees to access these services off-site. Green workplace services also have a positive impact on personal health and wellness. Naturally, if an employee is healthy, he or she will use fewer sick days and will be more productive. Some benefits promoting health include coverage of holistic medicine practices, such as acupuncture or massage. Others include fitness benefits, such as an on-site gym or discounts to a local fitness facility. Some companies look to provide green food opportunities, such as free fruit in the office or cafeterias serving locally grown and organic food.

Another way that a company's commitment to sustainability can benefit its employees is through the facility itself, particularly with regard to the indoor environmental quality of the workplace. Improvements in the facility can provide a desirable workplace that not only attracts and retains employees, but also increases their productivity. Additionally, the physical representation of a commitment to green is a benefit for many. Many companies opt to display their support of the environment by certifying the building's "green-ness" through an objective third party such as the USGBC's Leadership in Energy and Environmental Design (LEED) rating system. Other options include visible sustainable measures such as on-site composting, solar panels, wind farms, or green roofs.

Regardless of the options selected, companies are finding that green benefits play a big role in the process of attracting, hiring, and retaining the best employees. Google offers an impressive employee benefit package, with several options focused on health and the environment, including:

- Gourmet restaurants on-site, free for employees (saving money + no need to drive for meals = good for employee and the environment)
- Healthy snack rooms
- Free wi-fi equipped coach-style busses for employee transportation
- Subsidized on-site oil changes
- Gym on-site
- Subsidized exercise classes
- Massage room
- On-site child care
- Free access to plug-in hybrid cars to run errands during the day
- On-site physicians for employee checkups
- Motorized scooters and bikes to move between buildings

But your company does not have to be the size of Google to provide significant benefits to employees. For example, NRG Systems, a wind-measurement device maker in Hinesburg, Vermont, offers its eighty-five employees incentives to be more energy efficient and to use alternative energies at home and on the road.[13] NRG makes its money through wind energy, and its corporate leadership wanted to make sure they were walking the talk. Here are some of the many things NRG does for its employees:

- Hosts regular industry big-picture meetings in which one of the founders gives a fifteen-minute presentation on a topic relating the company's core activities to wider events and news items
- Brings in outside speakers to give an even wider perspective
- Offers a stipend of $300 per year to employees that can be used toward energy efficiency, such as compact fluorescent light bulbs, cleaning furnaces, or installing more energy-efficient windows
- Provides a company incentive for making green purchasing decisions called Clean NRG. This incentive program gives employees $1,000 per year toward a Toyota Prius, a solar hot-water system, solar panels, a wind turbine, or a wood-pellet furnace. If employees choose to buy a Prius, they get $1,000 per year toward that purchase as long as they own the vehicle. They can claim two items in any one year, or up to $2,000 annually. These benefits cost the company about $39,000 in 2006.

Seventy-six percent of employees took advantage of the NRG Systems energy-efficiency benefits in 2006 and roughly 30 percent took advantage of Clean NRG.

Greening the Recruiting Process

Once a company has established itself as a leader in sustainability and has begun to attract employees with a commitment to sustainability, it is time to address the recruiting process itself. To prove that your company really does practice sustainable behaviors, it is critical to have a consistent message throughout all phases of the recruiting process: advertisement; resume reception; recruiting events; interviews; and hiring.

One of the easiest ways to have a consistent message—as has been alluded to in some prior examples—is to shift to an online recruiting process. It is becoming standard practice to accept only electronic resumes that are either inputted directly into a database through a Web site or sent to human resources departments as PDF files. Taking the idea of going paperless a step further, companies might opt to shift their advertising online, focusing on relevant Web sites, social networking communities, typical recruiting sites, and online industry magazines. Any time paper is used as part of the recruiting process, it should be recycled, recyclable, or Forest Stewardship Council (FSC)-certified (and labeled as such).

Recruits do not expect their future employers to be perfect. But they do expect a certain amount of commitment and resources to be dedicated to understanding, developing, and implementing green strategies. Young recruits are surprisingly knowledgeable and should be seen as a resource to the organization. Tapping into their passion and energy on a regular basis can help the organization deliver better strategies and give these young people leadership opportunities that they need and crave.

A great example of a company that has figured this out is General Electric (GE). In 2006, they teamed up with mtvU, MTV's 24-hour college network, and offered U.S. college students the chance to win a $25,000 grant to develop an environmental project to implement on their own campus.[14] The contest, called the Ecomagination Challenge, fielded more than one hundred proposals. The winning team, from the Massachusetts Institute of Technology, took top honors for its solar-powered processor. Throughout the contest, a specially designed Web site detailed its progress and provided links to GE's online job application site. GE was not only able to recruit these students, but also got to see them in action.

If a new recruit is interviewed at your organization, how will he or she know that your green message is not greenwashing? Think about all of the ways that recruits come to you and then consider ways to thoughtfully incorporate your sustainable vision into the process of hiring. What does your Web site look like? Is your socially responsible message apparent? If you brought someone into your office for an interview, what would they see? Savvy green employees (and clients) will notice if you don't practice what you preach. Even the most trivial bad practices can speak volumes:

- Handing a recruit a Styrofoam coffee cup or a disposable plastic bottle
- Giving a recruit a big pile of paper marketing materials to review

- Not having a recycling bin in the kitchen
- Providing hand towels instead of air-dryers in the restroom

Also, during the interview, be sure to mention the green benefits offered by your company and the green training you provide to new employees. In fact, be sure to mention it a few times—it helps when more than one interviewer can vouch for the company's commitments to green initiatives.

Keeping Green Talent

It's not just recruits who are paying attention to their organization's environmental approach. Current employees are also aware of green workplace initiatives, and want to see their employer in the game. The Society for Human Resource Management (SHRM) survey mentioned earlier found that when employees working for organizations without environmentally responsible programs were asked if these programs were important, nearly three quarters (73 percent) of them said yes.[15]

A focus on recruiting new employees that are passionate about social or environmental issues is important, but some of the best green talent, and talent that can affect change, comes from within the organization. Current employees have the institutional knowledge, internal and external relationships, and credentials to bring "reality" to green ideas that help them stick. Ongoing training and enrollment of current employees increases employee awareness and taps into creative ideas that might not have surfaced otherwise. How do you do this?

- Try multiple channels, such as creating a green Web site or blog and sending out e-mail communications to promote ideas as they occur.
- Host "green" bag lunches (in person or virtually) and invite speakers to talk about the environment, especially as it relates to your industry.
- Ask different functional representatives within the organization to present to the office, and explain how they are playing their part to green your business.

- Encourage a few enthusiastic Greeniacs to create a short video showing "the day in the life of a green worker" in your office. Sometimes a picture really is worth a thousand words.

Now that you have your organizational structure in place and your employees and recruits engaged, what are some specific ways that you can green your business and your buildings? Take some time, think it through fully, and yes, keep reading. For once you are truly walking the talk, you'll find that recruits and employees alike will notice your green-ness—without you having to say a word.

Actions You Can Take Today

1. If you had to re-write your own job description to include incentives directed at your own green behavior, how would you change your own responsibilities and performance metrics? Now apply this same thinking to writing job descriptions for recruits.
2. Provide green benefits as incentives to individuals and teams and describe these "integrated" brand messages in recruiting materials.

Does your organization walk the talk? Take note of the embedded messages a new recruit to your office will pick up, everything from product and services literature to the impression left by the amount of paper lying around the office. Solicit help from your colleagues to change this.

CHAPTER 7

Leveraging Technology

Not all problems have a technological answer, but when they do, that is the more lasting solution.

—Andrew Grove, Hungarian-American businessman
and scientist, former CEO of Intel

The twenty-first century has brought about incredible innovations in technology, and the workplace has been affected by them in a profound way. Remember when faxing was "cutting edge?" Remember when the Internet was first popularized and you had to pay for it by the minute? Today we take these technologies for granted. They and many others like them are critical to the way we do business, and all indications are that technological innovation will only accelerate as we shape the workplaces of the future. Consider the impacts of using computer interfaces like those Tom Cruise's character used in the movie *Minority Report*—pulling up documents and then sorting, editing, and filing them in thin air. Or the virtual "hologram" used by CNN's Anderson Cooper to interview Will.i.am on the night of the 2008 U.S. presidential election. While you might not have seen these, believe it or not, early prototypes of *both* of these technologies are in existence today, and have the potential to dramatically change how and where people work.

In addition to changing the nature of our work, technology is a particularly powerful tool for combating environmental problems. It enables individuals, organizations, and other communities to collaborate and innovate remotely and on a global scale. It can also make our buildings smarter and more efficient through such automated measures as keeping the lights and the heating, ventilation, and air conditioning (HVAC) running only when needed. In fact, new applications of such green-enabling technology are emerging every day. In some corporate elevator lobbies, for example, employees waiting to ride an elevator enter the destination floor on an elevator call panel. The panel then displays a car number to ride, using a building-specific algorithm programmed to group riders and minimize the number of trips.

Enabling More Efficient and Effective Work

The cellular telephone, or cell phone, has afforded us the ability to communicate with practically anyone, at anytime. It is one of the more impactful technologies of recent decades. But this is just one of the many technological breakthroughs that have changed how we can now work more effectively and in an environmentally friendly way.

For example, many new technologies are enabling far greater mobility and distance work, improving the efficiency of employees, and allowing corporate real-estate managers to reduce property holdings. Other technologies help teams work together more effectively in remote situations, thereby reducing the need for travel and the resulting carbon dioxide from transportation emissions. Still other technologies allow employees to share documents virtually, eliminating the need for paper (and shipping that paper from one office to another). These technologies are described below:

Telephony

Telephony has come a long way since the days of Alexander Graham Bell when telephones were connected directly in pairs. Now the rotary phones with the long tangled cords and the "bag phones" we carried in our cars are ancient history. Telephony has long been and remains a critical element of a successful business, keeping workers connected with their colleagues and, of course, their clients and customers. As the options for telephony have expanded and gone mobile, the ability of companies to stay connected globally has increased dramatically.

This increase in connectivity and mobility can help companies green their operations in a range of ways. First, they can decrease the number of electronic devices required (primarily due to the rapidly expanding definition of what a "phone" is—computer, camera, video recorder, etc.). Also, given that employees are far better able to work from anywhere (well, nearly anywhere), this can help reduce the need for transportation—fewer trips to the office, to find a pay phone, etc. As with all new technology, there are some environmental negatives, such as the fact that all these devices still require energy to run and must regularly be updated. Whenever new products are generated and old ones are disposed, there is an environmental impact. This should be considered when acquiring new technologies and tech devices for your business, and of course when getting rid of old ones.

Examples of especially relevant telephony technologies in use today include:

- *Cell phones.* Cell phones allow employees to be connected from anywhere with reception (home, airport, hotel, other office sites, etc.). If you are looking for ways to green your cell phone, there are hundreds of fashionable solar chargers on the market that have taken the form of backpacks, purses, and jackets. Go ahead and make a statement! Also, turn it off when you aren't using it to save battery life.
- *Voice over Internet Protocol (VoIP) and Internet Protocol Telephony (IPT).* VoIP is an optimized protocol that enables the transmission of voice through the Internet or other packet switched networks. VoIP allows users to make calls directly from a computer, a special VoIP phone, or a traditional phone connected to a special adapter. VoIP can be accessed by a high-speed Internet connection, either wirelessly or through a local area network (LAN) line. IPT is a term often used interchangeably with VoIP. However, VoIP just accommodates voice whereas IPT accommodates voice as well as text, fax, and other services. Services such as Vonage, Skype, and Google Talk are examples of IPT.

- *Follow-Me.* This type of system enables the user to input a variety of phone numbers into the system (work phone, cell phone, home phone, etc.). When a call arrives, the follow-me system will try each number on the list until someone answers. If there is no answer, the call is transferred to a centralized phone-mail system that can be checked from any phone or over the Internet. This type of system enables greater mobility and ease of connection, and you don't have to keep three or more phone numbers with you as you travel.

- *Non-Assigned Private Branch Exchange (PBX) Phone.* A PBX phone is a telephone exchange that serves a particular business or office, and connects the internal lines to a Public Switched Telephone Network (PSTN) through trunk lines. Each end point on a PBX system (phone, fax, modem, etc) is typically referred to as an extension. A nonassigned PBX phone supplies phones with no owners. When a user arrives, he or she uses a dynamic login to the phone itself, meaning that any phone can have your number. In the case of many workplaces—especially those with staggered shifts—this can mean a reduced need for individual phones.

Computing technology

Remember when personal computers took up an entire room? Or, if you are too young to remember that, do you remember when they took up your entire desk? In just a few short decades, computers have become infinitely smaller, more powerful, more portable, and require less material to make and energy to run. Examples include:

- *Laptops.* Laptop computers have grown in both power and popularity. A typical laptop uses half the energy required by a desktop and in some cases up to 80 percent less energy.[1] For additional savings, enable the sleep mode on your laptop after five minutes of inactivity. If you have a desktop computer with an old cathode ray tube (CRT) monitor, consider replacing it with a liquid crystal display (LCD) screen. A fourteen-inch LCD monitor uses up to 75 percent less energy than its CRT equivalent.

- *Thin Client.* A thin client is a low-cost, centrally managed computer without a hard disk drive, CD-ROM players, disk drives, or other expansion slots. These computers are typically limited to performing only essential applications, as the majority of software and data is located on a server. Thin clients are typically less vulnerable to computer viruses, have a longer life cycle, use less power, and are less expensive. Additionally, users do not "own" a thin client computer. Any user can log on to any machine and access the same programs and data.

- *Personal Digital Assistant (PDA).* PDAs are small, handheld computers that have many uses: calculator, calendar, word processing, and address book, to name just a few. PDAs have become much more advanced over the last decade and are now typically integrated with cellular telephone and Internet services, such as the Treo and BlackBerry models. These devices have allowed workers to be in constant communication with clients and colleagues without using the energy required by a PC or laptop. As Don Horn from the General Services Administration (GSA) points out, BlackBerrys have "helped my team be more informed and communicating all the time. These devices have helped with communications, time management, and responsibility management."[2]

VIRTUAL MEETINGS

Meeting virtually is an especially impactful way for employers to go green, while saving time, travel, and paper. Virtual meetings can incorporate teleconferencing, videoconferencing, Web conferencing, electronic whiteboards, or a host of other technologies.

- *Teleconference.* Teleconferencing enables simultaneous conference calls to multiple sites distributed via audio, typically over a telephone connection. This can be accomplished through the conferencing capabilities of a standard desk phone, or through a teleconferencing service that allows the host to send a toll-free number and password to a practically unlimited number of users.

- *Videoconference.* Videoconferencing facilitates communication between participants at two or more locations who are linked by fast telecommunication lines and are able to see and hear one another in real time. There are numerous types of videoconferencing hardware and software systems. Truly advanced videoconferencing facilities, such as Cisco's TelePresence or Hewlett Packard's HALO technology, are carefully designed to enhance visual and sound quality to simulate "real life," and are set up in rooms designed to make participants feel as though they are all seated at the same conference table.

- *Web conference.* Web conferencing can take on many formats, with the basic underlying principle that attendees are linked through an Internet interface. They can work well for both planned and spontaneous remote collaboration. In some instances, Web conferences are a text-only interface, essentially, managed chat rooms. Others may include teleconference, video conference, or sharing of documents, video and multimedia. Some of the most popular choices include Net Meeting, GoToMeeting, WebEx, or Live Meeting. These systems can be used for many functions, such as sharing presentations, documents, video, and multimedia, demonstrating products, and viewing other user desktops.

- *Electronic whiteboards.* We've come a long way since the blackboard. New technologies on the collaboration front allow teams to "show" each other what they are working on electronically and interact with the content remotely. Products like Mimio, Polyvision, Teamspot, and Thunder are redefining and enhancing the experience of remote conferencing. Many of these products can display data from any source (computer files, scanned images, video images, or handwritten notes and sketches) both in the room and remotely. With some products, the displayed files can be edited in real time by local and remote users. The data from the meeting can be easily captured and stored for ongoing development, or distributed automatically by e-mail.

VIRTUAL KNOWLEDGE MANAGEMENT

The Internet, while an incredible tool for sharing information on a massive scale, is also slowly taking away the need for "libraries" of information in

The Impact of Travel

It's worth weighing not only the cost of travel in your organization, but also the environmental impact. If you are a frequent international traveler, your impact is significant. For example, HOK recently looked at the possibility of a four-person team flying to the Middle East from the U.S. East Coast for a project. The carbon footprint for flights alone was 2.4 metric tons of carbon dioxide per person for a round trip. To put this in perspective, the average U.S. citizen contributes 19.4 metric tons of carbon dioxide in a whole year,[3] and the global average is 4 metric tons.

Then HOK considered the economic costs. For the four people on the team, including four flights, three nights each in a hotel, taxis, and meals, expenses would be close to $40,000. Adding on the twenty-two hours of pure travel time per person multiplied by average hourly billing rates increased costs to close to $55,000. The other costs considered were opportunity costs (the team had to miss several marketing meetings to go) as well as costs to family (such as missed soccer games and family dinners). When HOK combined all trips made by employees domestically and globally as a firm in 2007, travel turned out to be over 53 percent of the company's entire carbon footprint and a significant cost to the bottom line. Senior leaders quickly decided to invest in high-quality video and electronic whiteboard technology across 20 locations. It was not a difficult business case to make.

hard copy. Its ability to retrieve information quickly allows workers to free themselves from paper copies of resources they needed in the past. Even the Library of Congress (LOC), the largest library in the world in terms of shelf space, is embracing the digital revolution. Specifically, the LOC is making impressive strides on its Web archives, composed of collections of archived Web sites selected by subject specialists to represent Web-based information on a designated topic. It is part of a continuing effort by the LOC to evaluate, select, collect, catalog, provide access to, and preserve digital materials for future generations of researchers.

VIRTUAL TRAINING

Organizations spend millions training new and existing employees each year. Sometimes this can only be done face-to-face, but a growing number

of companies see the financial (and environmental) benefits of virtual training. For instance, AT&T now uses the Internet extensively for training purposes. Classroom training still exists but it is used only for those subject areas
where it is absolutely necessary. Some companies are moving toward a more
blended approach to merge classroom training, "live" training using tools
like WebEx, and on-demand recorded training, with each mode comple-
menting the other. For example, a course that was formerly two weeks of
classroom training might now consist of eight days of Internet-based training followed by a two-day class. Instructors can travel to the students in this
type of arrangement, saving vast amounts of travel costs and classroom space.

Reducing the need for paper

There are many ways to leverage the software you already have in order to reduce paper use: for example, by simply making double-sided printing the
default setting for your printer, by reviewing documents electronically, or
using larger monitors so that there is less need to print.

Some companies have taken the concept of going digital even further.
Sprint, for example, has developed an entire program around leveraging digital technology. In 2005 the company started iDigitize, a training program
managed by the technology component of Sprint's real-estate organization.
This program was crucial to helping staff become more mobile—which was
one goal—but it had the added benefit of saving a great deal of paper. Sprint's
iDigitize program combined Sprint technology and a combination of strategies to become more mobile, save paper, and above all save costs.[4] Here's a
sampling of the components of the program:

- Accessing Sprint e-mail from any computer using Webmail
- Using the Sprint Intranet from a Sprint laptop outside the office
- Using Sprint's wireless access
- Checking e-mail using a Sprint wireless device
- Instant Messaging (as part of Microsoft's communication package)
- Audio conferencing
- Virtual face-to-face meetings via video teleconferencing

- Small, impromptu online meetings (Live Meeting)
- Large, prescheduled online meetings (Sprint Meeting Place)
- Archiving hardcopy documents as digital copies by scanning
- Sending faxes from computer (Webfax)
- Receiving faxes via computer (Bizcom Fax)
- Using black-and-white print as standard default
- Setting company default to two-sided printing

Implementing steps such as these led to a paper reduction of 12 percent for Sprint in 2006 and 20 percent in 2007. The program was a comprehensive one, focused on reaching employees in a range of ways. It involved a branded program, a Web site, and an extensive training program for all employees. A large part of this initiative focused on the importance of the environment, but increasing productivity—spending less time trying to figure out how tools work, and more time using them—was also paramount.

Sprint's pitch for using digital technology—especially instead of paper— was direct, focused, and specific to the company itself:

- The value of every employee gaining five minutes of productivity per day = $40 million
- Every Sprint employee printing ten fewer pages per week = $750K savings annually and saving 3,600 trees
- Reducing overall printing at Sprint by 25 percent = $3 million savings annually
- Ten percent of employees taking one less business trip per year = $6 million savings annually

Often, the reason green workplace technologies are not used more is because employees don't know how to use them or aren't aware of their benefits. The most successful strategies are those that are easy to implement and increase awareness at the same time. An example of this is Greenprint, a software package that automatically removes blank pages from your documents prior to printing. If you set Greenprint as your default printer, it shows you an "at a glance" view of your entire document and automatically highlights the pages or images you might want to delete prior to printing. Users actually "see" the amount of paper they are saving, which increases their awareness of the amount of paper they print on a regular basis. The program also comes with a little meter to tell the user how much paper and ink is saved when the user chooses not to print blank pages. This meter creates an incentive to improve performance over time.

Mass Collaboration

We're finally catching on to the power of the Internet to enable mass collaboration. It is now home not just to straightforward Web sites, but to social networking services, blogs, wikis, shared video, instant messaging, and a whole host of other tools that allow people to connect to each other and create ideas in new ways. One of the most powerful ways of implementing green strategies with technology is by *using these tools to innovate.* In *Wikinomics,* Don Tapscott and Anthony Williams refer to these tools as "weapons of mass collaboration." They claim that "new low-cost collaborative infrastructures— from free Internet telephony to open source software to global outsourcing platforms—allow thousands upon thousands of individual and small producers to co-create products, access markets, and delight customers in ways that only larger corporations could manage in the past."[5] Here are a few favorite enablers of collaboration that have been especially influential for business and the environmental movement:

SOCIAL NETWORKING

Social networking tools build online communities of people who share common interests and activities, or are researching the interests and activities of others. Social networking Web sites, like Facebook, LinkedIn, MySpace, Orkut, Twitter, and Cyworld have created powerful new ways to communicate and share information, and are being used regularly by millions of people. It now seems that social networking will be an enduring part of everyday life. The great news for environmentalists is that they can share information with a wide audience quickly and cheaply. Social networks also naturally stimulate communities of people to have a focused discussion around solving environmental problems.

Virtual worlds

Virtual worlds are three-dimensional social networking sites that allow the user to interact as an "avatar" or three-dimensional (3D) character in a modeled virtual universe. Examples include Second Life, Kaneva, and Entropia Universe. Although the 3D models are still a little rough, this hasn't stopped a number of companies from "buying islands" or virtual space in these worlds and using them for business purposes. Companies and organizations like Autodesk, Crown Plaza, McKinsey, Bain and Company, Harvard Law School, and the U.S. Centers for Disease Control are some of the many users. There is a short learning curve to use the software, which is more interactive and exploratory than traditional communication media. Organizations now use virtual worlds to educate, to communicate with their staff and shareholders, to host conferences, to try new products in a low-risk environment, and to brand their products and services in a new way. How are virtual worlds environmentally friendly?

- There is no need to travel to Boston to take a class at Harvard, to jet off to Tokyo for a business meeting, or even to go into the office at all. Your avatar walks into a virtual room and communicates with others in real time, and you do everything from your laptop.
- There is the potential to "model" products, buildings, games, and other 3D objects and to test them prior to investing physical resources. University of California–Irvine computer scientist Crista Lopes built a virtual model of a rapid-transit system called SkyTran in Second Life, with software to keep SkyTran's virtual cars from getting into virtual collisions. After the control software is ready in Second Life, she plans to transfer it to a real-world version of SkyTran, proposed by the Irvine-based transportation company Unimodal, Inc. Using virtual software like Second Life helped iron out issues that could only have been discovered by "experiencing" the design. One such issue, for example, was the alignment of the express track

directly over the platform, which is technically safe, but was judged to feel unsafe by Second Life users. The second issue arose from the clear "glass" used in the Second Life pods. Unimodal officials responded that, if this material were used in a real-life SkyTran pod, it could expose passengers to a fast, repetitive pattern of SkyTran track components moving by, which could produce epileptic seizures in some people.[6]

WIKI TECHNOLOGY

A wiki is a page or collection of Web pages designed to enable anyone who accesses it to contribute or modify content using a simplified markup language. The collaborative encyclopedia Wikipedia is one of the best-known examples. Wikis are used in business to provide Intranets and Knowledge Management systems. The power of this technology is only just now being tapped into, but, given the complexity of environmental issues, tools like these will be critical to understanding issues and building consensus around solutions in the future. Some of the organizations exploring wiki technology are surprising:

- The United Nations (UN), notorious for endless deliberations, is looking to technology to help facilitate consensus. Its Global Compact Office, which promotes corporate social responsibility, has embraced the wiki in hopes that it will help staff in eighty countries share information and reach common understanding with less deliberation and more speed. This project intends to review and tag thousands of separately generated UN reports so that they are searchable and more easily accessible.
- IBM has used internal wikis since 2005, with the intention of selling the concept to its clients. IBM has incorporated the wiki and other collaborative software into its corporate products like Lotus Notes, a desktop software for accessing e-mail and other applications.
- Sixteen U.S. intelligence agencies have begun using a common wiki called Intellipedia, a government-run—and top-secret—information-sharing source that allows them to merge research and intelligence gathering.
- WikiCongress, powered by Rally Communications and founded by former U.S. congressional staffers, is slightly different from traditional

wiki technology. It lets the public create petitions or propose new policies and then forwards the results to legislators. WikiCongress also includes a Facebook application so that petitions can be signed through Facebook.[7]

MASS-COLLABORATION TECHNOLOGIES like social networking and wikis are incredibly powerful in the sense that they enable many people to share ideas at the same time and self-correct information. This is particularly important given the enormous amount of environmentally related information being produced and the prevalence of greenwashing.

Technology Influencing Behavior

Changing behavior is one of the greatest challenges to successfully rolling out a green strategy. However, technology can help here as well. Organizations

How This Book Was Written

This book started out as a blog (www.TheGreenWorkplace.com) in November 2007. Initially the blog was written by just a handful of contributors, but soon many more partners and clients were added, up to a total of roughly 25 writers. The content also grew quickly—from just a few posts to hundreds—covering a range of topics including carbon offsets, design ideas, green recruiting, energy policy, new technology, and the like, all within about three months. It eventually became a repository for many of the issues, ideas, and examples in this book. It hosts many of the public links to articles and resources used to research the book. The blog is similar to a wiki in the sense that it collected a large body of information that is self-corrected by both the bloggers and anyone using the Internet who chooses to comment on it.

If this book had been written twenty years ago, it would have taken three times as long to write with countless trips to the library. Instead, most of the research documents needed were accessible online, so they could be quickly scanned (again, electronically) to find relevant content. The resources used were from reputable, validated sources, but the way those sources were initially discovered was often through Web searches, listservs (short for electronic mailing list servers), blogs, and wikis.

are increasingly looking to software applications and other tools to educate, motivate, and remind individuals or groups why their behavior can either help or hurt the environment. Typically, such tools do some combination of the following:

- Identify why certain actions are better for the environment than others
- Help determine the impact of actions such as measuring the real-time "status" of energy use or greenhouse gas emissions
- Provide historical information and predict future trends
- Compare people to their neighbors, friends, colleagues, or people of the same demographic

So much of being a good steward of the environment is about being aware of and understanding the impacts of individual actions. But collecting an accurate picture of one's carbon footprint or energy use requires an almost obsessive focus on measurement. Most people may try to do the right thing, but do not have time or energy to evaluate the "greenness" of every decision they make on a consistent basis. That is where technology comes into play—helping make people aware of the impact of their actions and motivating them to adjust behavior. Here are some particularly effective motivators.

Saving money

There are a number of ways that technology can influence behavior by tying environmentally beneficial behavior to cost savings. For example, some insurance companies are now offering "pay as you drive" car insurance. The insurance company will put a global positioning system (GPS) tag on your car so that the insurer knows precisely how far you drive—which, in combination with your safe driving record, determines your premium. The state of California now allows drivers to buy these auto insurance policies, which provide an incentive to reduce unnecessary driving. The Brookings Institution suggests that nearly two-thirds of California households would have lower rates under this system because drivers would drive less, with the average savings per household coming to $276 a year.[8]

INCREASING AWARENESS

Technologies that increase awareness of individual environmental impact can be enough to help those same individuals change their ways. National Grid, a UK-based utility company, recently launched a new virtual application, Floe. Floe, a virtual polar bear on National Grid's Web site (www.nationalgridfloe.com), can help National Grid customers analyze and measure the environmental effects of their routine daily activities, including eating, drinking, driving, and making home-heating energy choices. Visitors interact with Floe and learn how positive environmental acts will help protect the environment. Users learn how the energy choices we make and the actions we take make a positive or negative difference on the environment. Every time the user does something that benefits the environment—such as using energy-efficient products, reusable shopping bags, or taking showers instead of baths—the iceberg on the visitor's Web page grows. People can even adopt, name, and interact with a virtual polar bear—feeding it fish, playing with a ball, and watching it grow.

In addition to showing users how to reduce their carbon footprint, the Floe site provides links to National Grid energy efficiency programs and services as well as energy information and tips from various sources. There is a community message board on which consumers can post comments regarding actions they are taking to reduce their impact on climate change and see what others are doing in their region.

SOCIAL INFLUENCE

Some of the most interesting technology solutions are based on the research of Dr. Robert Cialdini and other social psychologists who have proven the strong connection between social influence and human behavior. Positive Energy, a software company, is working with Dr. Cialdini to develop customized energy reports. The reports take utility information and send customers personalized energy use data through a regular newsletter. The newsletter provides customers detailed information about their own energy consumption, but also compares them to their other residents and to "ideal" citizens *in their neighborhoods.* The result? Time and time again, a direct

Social Influence on Campus

Oberlin College

A group of researchers and students at Oberlin College did a study to assess how socio-technical feedback, combined with incentives, might encourage students to conserve resources. They set up an automated data monitoring system that provided dormitory residents with real-time Web-based feedback on their energy usage. In contrast, utility meters were manually read for twenty other dormitories, and data was provided to those residents just once per week. For both groups, resource use was monitored during a baseline period and during a two-week "dorm energy competition" during which feedback, education, and conservation incentives were provided.

Overall, the introduction of feedback, education, and incentives resulted in a 32 percent reduction in electricity use. However, dormitories that received the real-time feedback were far more effective at conservation, reducing their electricity consumption by 55 percent, compared to 31 percent for dormitories that only received feedback once a week.[9]

The group of students who did this study went on to create Lucid Design Group, a company that uses this technology for other colleges and universities as well as corporate campuses.[10]

comparison *to people like them* was far more effective in reducing energy consumption than communications that did not provide the comparison.

This link between technology and behavior is a particularly strong one, given the fact that people are often unaware of how their actions are affecting the environment. Changing behavior takes practice and constant reminding—and technology can help us in a way that is non-threatening and even fun.

Smart Buildings

Building automations systems (BAS) are effectively control systems that keep the building climate within a specified range, provide lighting based on an occupancy schedule, monitor system performance and device failures, and provide e-mail or text notifications to building engineering staff. The BAS functionality reduces building energy and maintenance costs when compared to a non-controlled building. A building controlled by a BAS is often referred to as an intelligent or smart building system.

There is a convergence happening between information technology (IT) and traditional building technology. As BAS technology improves, it is being integrated with traditional IT infrastructures. Building systems are beginning to share data, but are also linking up with other business applications, improving efficiency and real-time control over building operating costs. At Panasonic Corporation of North America's headquarters, for example, a project is underway to replace wall-mounted thermostats (traditionally a building control) with individual, virtual thermostats controlled by personal computers.[11] And this is just the start. Here are some other examples of where we are headed when it comes to cutting-edge technology and building management:

BUILDING INFORMATION MODELING

Over the years, architects and engineers have moved from hand-drawing buildings to designing buildings using software or computer aided design (CAD) tools that create a series of two-dimensional (2D) sketches. The new tool for drawing is called Building Information Modeling (BIM), a digital, 3D model of a building that is linked to a database of project information. Some describe BIM, at its heart, as a database in the visual form of a "virtual building." BIM can combine, among other things, the design, fabrication information, erection instructions, and project management logistics into one database. It is also a platform for collaboration throughout the project's design and construction. And because the model and database can exist for the life of a building, the owner can use BIM to manage the facility well beyond the completion of construction for such purposes as space planning, furnishing, long-term energy performance and energy recovery, maintenance, carbon dioxide monitoring, and remodeling.[12]

That said, BIM is an evolving technology and is not used consistently in the construction industry at the present time because it takes significant training to use effectively. However, as it is adopted further over time, it promises to bring with it many economic and environmentally friendly advantages:

- Better visualization. Because these models are created in 3D, it is much easier for the client and design team to work through issues early—well before construction begins.
- Ability to "model" scenarios. The ability of these systems to quickly generate models of walls, air handling units, electrical conduits, and even furniture allows the design team to reduce material use and make more environmentally friendly choices. This is similar to the 3D modeling the University of California–Irvine did in Second Life simulating SkyTran, only using a more complex "layering" of data required for effectively designing, constructing, and managing buildings.
- Fewer coordination errors. Many of the problems that plague building construction stem from the fact that various disciplines have trouble communicating with one another—particularly regarding changes in materials, approach, and scope. At its core, BIM facilitates the sharing of information among these disciplines and reduces the number of errors that result from insufficient communication.
- More efficient scheduling and reduced construction time. This improved communication will allow project managers to establish and adjust schedules more accurately and precisely and to shave precious time from work schedules.

Managing building utilization

This may surprise you, but even during work hours, office buildings are only partially occupied most of the time. Analysis shows that for corporate and government administrative facilities, less than half of workers are actually sitting at their desks (typically around 40 to 50 percent of desks are occupied even during peak use) during a typical nine-hour workday. Employees are working from home, visiting clients, traveling or "flash commuting" somewhere besides their office. Tools that can either increase utilization or reduce the energy required to heat and cool these buildings can make a big impact. Here are two examples:

- PeopleCube is an office scheduling software that recently began selling its system as a way to allocate "hoteling" or "hot-desk" space inside companies where mobile workers might need a desk just for one day. They link the hot-desk scheduler into office buildings' environmental management systems, so that lighting, heating, or cooling can be adjusted to comfortable levels on floors where the hoteling space fills up and turned down to save energy on floors with a large percentage of empty cubicles. PeopleCube has partnered with a UK consultancy called Building Sustainability Ltd. (BSL) to add a "carbon dashboard" to the scheduler, so that facility managers can see exactly how much carbon dioxide emission is being avoided thanks to their scheduling efforts. PeopleCube's Resource Scheduler is used by over one hundred thousand employees at General Motors and eighty thousand at Procter & Gamble for reserving physical resources such as conference rooms, hoteling space, and teleconferencing facilities.[13]

- The Bick Group is a company in St. Louis that specializes in data center consulting, design, construction, and maintenance services. The company recently converted a former printing company facility into a green building that serves as its headquarters. As part of the process, it integrated various building systems onto a common software platform that allows building occupants to control their personal environment from their desktops. The building has sensors throughout that measure and automatically modulate temperature, humidity, air quality, and light levels based on interior and exterior conditions, occupancy, and amount of available daylight. Control systems automatically shut down HVAC and lighting at 6:00 p.m. to save energy; yet if occupants arrive during off hours, their access cards are integrated to turn on the lights and the HVAC system for their respective areas. Similarly, through a desktop interface, users who need to stay late at the office can click on a floor plan icon to reactivate the HVAC and lighting in their areas. To eliminate glare and help reduce the solar load on the HVAC system, window systems on the east and west exposures automatically react to exterior light levels as they track the sun across the sky. Should occupants wish to override the automatic position, an icon on the desktop allows them to do so. During the day software creates pop-up windows on occupants' desktops that suggest changes they can make to increase their thermal comfort. For example, a message pops up suggesting that occupants close the operable windows because of outside humidity or low air quality. Each workstation also has its own adjustable HVAC floor diffuser so that occupants can control their individual temperature. This combination of building design, systems integration, and a user-friendly desktop interface gives occupants awareness of the building conditions and the ability to control it as needed—a key element for worker productivity and satisfaction.[14]

Alternative Energy Technology

We have not mentioned alternative energy technologies (specifically, how they can support buildings or transportation). The technological innovation surrounding energy is so prolific today that it merits another book in itself, but suffice it to say that the green workplace is continually being improved through the integration of solar, wind, geothermal, wave technology, biodiesel, biomass, and the like. These energies are starting to be integrated into the building site, the building skin and structure, and into everything that makes up the "work" that happens within it, not to mention the changes in the auto industry.

One particularly compelling development that may have a profound impact on the workplace and beyond is the concept of the smart power grid. This "smart grid" is a transformed electricity transmission and distribution network that uses two-way communications, advanced sensors, and distributed computers to improve the efficiency, reliability, and safety of power delivery and use. It behaves much like the Internet in the sense that the Internet is a massive networking infrastructure that connects millions of computers together globally, forming a network in which any computer can communicate with any other computer. The smart grid proposes a similarly decentralized model where power distribution moves more efficiently through a large system of power sources rather than from centralized power plants. An example of an organization that is onboard with this concept is Gridpoint, a smart grid company that helps utility companies balance energy loads. The company has raised more than $220 million since its founding in 2003.[15] GridPoint's system helps convert energy from solar, wind, and other sources—installed at homes or businesses—into usable electricity, and automatically sells excess electricity to utilities at opportune times. Using software and communications with their network operations center, Gridpoint's energy management system can use weather forecasts and time-based pricing to make decisions about when to buy or sell. The system also enables utilities to balance supply and demand and avoid power outages by discharging stored power or reducing loads. Companies like Comverge, Consumer Powerline, EleQuant, EnerNOC, Fat Spaniel, and Silver Spring Networks also provide services for monitoring and managing the electric system and see tremendous market opportunity as well as environmental benefits from smart grid strategies.[16]

TECHNOLOGY IN GENERAL is changing so quickly that it is difficult to predict what new innovation will ultimately solve the environmental problems of today. However, waiting for something better to come along is not necessarily the right solution. Selectively purchasing green tools, testing them, training employees to use them, and then experimenting with what works best for your organizational culture will create the greatest environmental benefit. Even simple technology can be tailored to suit an individual's or company's needs—and it doesn't necessarily require new building construction or an operational overhaul. Technology can also be changed to adapt to human behavior or more stringent environmental targets over time.

Is technology alone the answer, when it comes to greening your workplace? No. But is it a powerful part of the solution? Unquestionably, yes.

Actions You Can Take Today

1. Do a quick audit of the software and hardware that you already have. What tools do you already own today that could help you manage your ecological footprint? For example, a number of PDAs have applications that track carbon emissions, fuel efficiency, avoid traffic jams, and find parking spots. Another step is to check the settings on your PC to ensure you use less paper: printing to PDF; double-sided printing; and printing in black-and-white rather than color are all environmentally friendly easy wins.

2. Scan documents and send e-mail rather than snail mail.
3. If your next meeting involves travel, figure out the cost of travel versus a tele- or video-conference. Some meetings are more important to have face-to-face than others, but don't let this be your default choice without really thinking it through.
4. Sign up for a listserv, newsgroup, blog, wiki, or community that will give you access to people with similar interests in the environment. Here are a few places to start:

    - Wikia Green (from the founder of Wikipedia): green.wikia.com/wiki/Wikia_Green
    - Great Green List (a list of listservs and other information): www.greatgreenlist.com
    - Greenversations (EPA's blog): blog.epa.gov/blog
    - Celsias (social network with community actions): www.celsias.com
    - The Green Workplace: *www.TheGreenWorkplace.com*

CHAPTER 8

Greening Operations

Use it up, wear it out, make it do, or do without.

—Old Saying

If you were going to build your company again from scratch, knowing what you now know about current environmental issues and concerns, how would you organize it differently? Would you change where your company is located? Who you hire? How you train them? The materials you use to build your buildings and products? The way you use energy and water? How you measure "success"?

Now think about how your company operates today. You may not have the luxury of starting from square one, but you can still make green decisions moving forward that will move your company closer to the ideal. Ray Anderson, the Founder and Chairman of Interface, Inc., tells the story about how his company turned around in his 1998 book, *Mid-Course Correction.* Anderson and his team made several changes in the way their business operated, creating a bold new vision of success: "To be the first company that, by its deeds, shows the entire industrial world what sustainability is in all its dimensions: People, process, product, place and profits—by 2020—and in doing so we will become restorative through the power of influence."[1]

Interface leadership looked at how they managed the life cycle of products and services throughout their business, including the purchase of supplies, the production of goods, the amount of waste created, and how they measured success. The process of reinventing themselves and the way they operated their business actually *increased* profits, while at the same time it reduced their environmental footprint dramatically. Anderson claims: "During the nine years we've been measuring it, the elimination of waste—the savings—represents 28 percent of our operating income, and we still have two-thirds of it yet to go. We've already captured about one-third. It gets close to doubling your profit if you can eliminate waste."[2] As your company develops its own environmental mission and sustainable operational strategies, look to companies like Interface that have already made strides in transforming their organization for inspiration and ideas. Here are some concepts and examples to catalyze greening the operations of your organization:

Measure Twice, Cut Once

The saying "measure twice, cut once" comes from the carpentry trade. Anyone who has taken up woodworking or a home improvement project knows to measure twice or more so as not to waste a good piece of wood: That can mean another trip to the hardware store, money down the drain, and a delay in completing a project. Creating and maintaining a sustainable workplace requires almost an obsession with measurement. This is difficult for most companies because they have vast experience tracking financial, human capital, or operational metrics but not environmental ones. Smart companies are not downplaying the importance of financial measures—especially in a global financial crisis when companies are downsizing and cost cutting whenever they can—but refining them to incorporate green costs and benefits, and thereby understand the full implications of their actions on the bottom line.

Most companies initiate their green makeover with an audit or commissioning process of some sort. The scope of the audit may include:

- Measuring key environmental parameters such as water use, energy use, and carbon dioxide emissions

- Analyzing and testing indoor and outdoor air quality, light metering, and water quality
- Reviewing purchase orders and invoices
- Inspecting facilities for materials used throughout
- Assessing the efficiency of thermal and lighting controls, and other building systems
- Interviewing employees, managers, and executives about environmental issues and opportunities for making improvements
- Communicating with contractors, vendors, customers, and regulators regarding their perception of the organization's environmental practices
- Examining policies, internal records, reports, and public statements relating to the environment
- Comparing audit results to previous audits, as well as to industry standards and best practices[3]

The benefits of an audit are many, including increased organizational awareness of issues that were unobserved in the past. But the most important outcome is a set of metrics and benchmarks that can be used as a baseline, and to establish later targets.

Establishing a baseline and monitoring operations over time provides a measure of environmental impact and suggests policies and procedures to meet environmental goals. For example, Adobe Systems, Inc. has taken measurement, particularly of its facilities, very seriously. In 2001, Adobe's real-estate group started to roll out energy-saving programs and began tracking progress. Adobe installed an operations system with real-time energy meters in its buildings that show not just energy usage, but also the carbon being generated and the cost. As soon as facilities management put the system on-line, the graphic display revealed several irregularities, including a "spike" in energy use. This was of particular concern as the utility bills were based on peak use during the day. Adobe found that the spike was due to multiple building systems starting up at once, so to minimize it, the company simply staggered when various systems started during the course of a day—eliminating the spikes, and reducing its bills considerably. According to Adobe, the real-time electricity meters paid for themselves in roughly six weeks.

Adobe also uses Smart ET for irrigation. These controllers monitor Evapo-Transpiration information from local weather stations and/or satellites and determine the amount of irrigation needed for landscaping. If the system senses a storm coming, it may choose to irrigate less, or not at all. Adobe has saved 76 percent of its water used for irrigation this way.[4]

Buying Wisely

Companies can wield a tremendous amount of power and influence through the act of purchasing wisely. To put this in perspective, of the one hundred largest "economies" in the world, fifty-one are corporations and only forty-nine are countries (based on a comparison of corporate sales and country gross domestic products [GDPs]). But it's not just size, it's also growth rate. The Top 200 corporations' sales are growing at a faster rate than overall global economic activity. Between 1983 and 1999, their combined sales grew from the equivalent of 25 to 27.5 percent of the world's GDP.[5] Their cumulative potential impact is staggering, especially considering that most of these corporations are just now adopting sustainability programs. But it's not just the biggest companies that can make a difference; any company can do its part. How? Key questions to ask when addressing procurement in the workplace are:

- Can you accommodate organizational needs *without* purchasing a particular product or service?
- Can you influence purchasing behavior by putting pressure on your suppliers?
- Can you change policies or protocols to impact operational or organizational behavior?

LESS IS MORE

The environmental impact of purchasing goods and services comes not from what companies spend, but from what they choose *not* to spend. Some of the most creative and environmentally friendly choices are those that involve solutions about occupying less space, buying fewer materials, and doing more with less. For example, it is common for many companies to use bottled water, Styrofoam or plastic cups, disposable plates and plastic silverware in every break room, café, or cafeteria. The ongoing costs of purchasing and recycling or disposing of these items is high, particularly over the long term, and the environmental impact is not so hot either. Each of these products requires a tremendous amount of material, water, and energy to produce and many of them release toxins into the environment during the manufacturing process, after they have been disposed of in a landfill, or during their incineration. Many companies have now made the decision to make a one-time purchase of water filters, silverware, china, and a few extra dishwashers to save costs and take plasticware and Styrofoam out of their waste stream entirely. As mentioned earlier, Sprint eliminated the use of 4.6 million foam cups annually, resulting in an annual savings of $135,000.[6]

LEVERAGE PARTNERSHIPS

One of the fastest ways to green business operations is to put the burden on suppliers. United Technologies Corporation (UTC), the eighteenth largest manufacturer in the United States, specializing in high-tech services to the aerospace and building industries, has an extensive reach, with a supply chain that includes more than fifty thousand companies with whom they spent a total of more than $20 billion in 2006. While UTC's sourcing decisions have always been based on the supplier's ability to provide high-quality products, UTC is now incorporating further expectations in the areas of environment, health, and safety. But it's not just about telling suppliers what to do; it's about finding sustainable partners who are ahead of you and finding what you can learn from them.

And you don't have to be the size of UTC to make demands on your partners. When the Wilderness Society renewed its lease in Washington, D.C., it was able to partner with its landlord, Boston Properties, who agreed as part of the negotiation to become carbon neutral. As a result, Boston Properties bought carbon credits for all their corporate office space across the country for the duration of the twelve-year lease.[7]

Sandy Thomaes, Corporate Real Estate Senior Consultant with a Canadian financial institution says, "Our strength is in the people that we work with. They make recommendations and we listen to them." The financial institution asked all of its vendors to draft green policies, and then turned this around and built these policies into its own contracts. The company's new environmentally responsible procurement guidelines are fairly comprehensive and include early education on life cycle costs.[8] These were implemented fully in 2007 and are now used to contract everything from architects and furniture providers to janitorial, heating, ventilation, and air conditioning (HVAC), and lighting services. Sustainable requirements are listed as a checklist in every request for proposal and include business practices, as well as the products and services that are provided.[9]

REDEFINE THE NEED

Vendors can help to diagnose the environmental problems you face. Sometimes they have a better insight as to where the issues lie, as organizations often ask the wrong questions when procuring products or services. Under its Evergreen Services Agreement, for example, Interface no longer sells carpet in the traditional sense, but rather leases a floor-covering service for a monthly fee, accepting responsibility for keeping the carpet fresh and clean. Monthly inspections detect and replace worn carpet tiles. Since, at most, 20 percent of an area typically shows at least 80 percent of the wear (usually in high-traffic areas), replacing only the worn parts reduces the consumption of carpeting material by about 80 percent. It also minimizes the disruption that customers experience—worn tiles are seldom found under furniture. For the customer, leasing carpets can provide a tax advantage by turning a capital expenditure into tax-deductible expense. Customers of leased carpet services receive cheaper and better services and the supplier has far less to produce.[10] All of this is good news for the environment, because there is less overall demand for materials, and energy and water to produce more carpet. It's a very clever approach for all involved, but realistically, what customer would even possibly have the knowledge to ask for such an approach, if their vendor, Interface, hadn't raised it in the first place?

So how can your organization flex the power of its green purchasing muscle? Insist that your suppliers disclose their carbon footprint, provide verifiable or third-party eco labels on their products (Green Seal, Energy Star, USDA Organic), and clearly explain how their product is produced:

- How much pre- and post-consumer recycled content does it have?
- Does it use bio-based materials?
- Was it locally made or transported from elsewhere?
- How is it packaged?
- What are the conditions of the factories where it was made or assembled?

In essence, your suppliers should be responding to the very same questions you are asking and should adopt your organization's priorities if they want to do business with you. And again, don't assume you have all the answers, or even the right questions. If the vendors and suppliers have further ideas on how to green your business together even more—listen to them.

Purchase Renewable Energy or Invest in Carbon Offsets

Environmentalists are not especially fond of purchasing offsets of any kind. They claim this is a way of avoiding "doing the right thing" to become carbon or energy neutral. Most companies, however, are not carbon or energy neutral now, nor will they be for a long time. Often this is because of issues with infrastructure or other influences that are out of the immediate control of the organization, such as limited access to renewable energy or mass transportation. Thus, purchasing offsets can often be the easiest way to make a real impact. To maximize the impact of offsetting, however, companies are thinking about ways to increase the impact of carbon emissions beyond just writing a check. Burt's Bees, the North Carolina-based producer of eco-friendly creams and cleansers, is encouraging its workers to support a green lifestyle by becoming carbon neutral in their personal lives. Toward that end, Burt's Bees is subsidizing its employees' purchases of renewable energy certificates. The employee subsidy is akin to a company offering matching contributions to a charity chosen by the employee. Burt's Bees hopes to eventually use only renewable energy in the future, but until technology improves and more renewable energy sources are available, the company has committed a sizable sum through its corporate and employee commitments to subsidize wind-energy production and offset its annual energy usage.[11]

Saving Energy and Water

Energy has taken a front seat in recent political and economic discussions and reducing energy use is probably one of the first actions that companies and individuals can do to reduce costs and impact their carbon footprint. Water, or access to potable water, is not as "urgent" in many regions of the world, but it is a serious concern overall and will certainly become more costly in the future. The good news is that strategies for reducing energy and water can be implemented throughout an organization by groups or individuals at any time. Some require a bit more planning, but some are quite easy. Key to all of them is increased communication and education about the great strategies already being used and potential future opportunities.

INCREASE AWARENESS AND ENCOURAGE PARTICIPATION

Here is a sampling of strategies that impact the bottom line and are effective at work and at home. Most of these strategies are low-tech and just good common sense:

- Replace incandescent light bulbs with compact fluorescent (CFL) or light-emitting diode (LED) bulbs for desk lamps and overhead lighting.
- Switch off all unnecessary lights. Use dimmers, motion sensors, or occupancy sensors to automatically turn off lighting when not in use to reduce energy use and costs.
- Use natural lighting or day lighting. When feasible, turn off lights near windows.
- Use task lighting (smaller lights near your work surface). Instead of brightly lighting an entire room, focus the light where you need it, to directly illuminate work areas.

- Use energy efficient ENERGY STAR or energy-rated products.

- Close or adjust window blinds to block direct sunlight, which will reduce cooling needs during warm months. Overhangs or exterior window covers are most effective to block sunlight on south-facing windows.

- Unplug equipment that drains energy when not in use (i.e., your computer, monitor, cell phone chargers, fans, coffeemakers, desktop printers, radios, etc.) Alternatively, use green power strips that are on a timer so that you will remember to turn things off.

- Turn off photocopiers at night or, when appropriate, purchase new copiers with a low power standby feature. Purchase printers and fax machines with a power management feature and use it.

- In the winter months, open blinds on south-facing windows during the day to allow sunlight to naturally heat your workspace. Close the blinds to reduce heat loss at night.

- Have a qualified professional perform an energy audit. Check with your utility company for names of auditors.

- Verify that the energy management system switches into setback mode during unoccupied hours.

- Install meters or sub-meters (if your office is in a building with other tenants) to track energy and water use.

- When driving any vehicle (yours or the company's), drive the speed limit, accelerate and decelerate slower, and make sure tires are fully inflated.

- Check for leaks in taps, pipes, and hoses to reduce water waste.

- Encourage employees to wait until they have a full load in the dishwasher before using it. This saves water and energy, and reduces the amount of detergent entering the sewer system.

- Rinsing dishes in a plugged sink or bowl rather than under a running tap saves water and is just as easy and effective.

- Use potable water only when needed for health or safety reasons.

- Consider installing your own wastewater treatment system to recycle water and cut down on water bills.

- Use low flow taps or tap aerators.

- Install dual-flush toilets.

CONTROL YOUR ENERGY USE

Many organizations make the mistake of thinking that utility costs are some-thing they cannot control or negotiate. In fact, there are many opportunities to take control of energy and water use. For example, leases are generally written for normal building hours, Monday through Friday from 8:00 a.m. to 7:00 p.m. for HVAC, security, and lighting, and from 8:00 a.m. to 2:00 p.m. on Saturday. Boston Properties, a self-administered and self-managed real estate investment trust, partners with their customers from the begin-ning of the lease negotiation process throughout the tenant's lease term to manage energy consumption. They let their clients know that, if they are not working Saturday hours, the building can be shut off most of the day (and turned on by individuals as needed). Boston Properties has achieved better than a 70 percent participation rate in just this one initiative across its nearly ten million square foot real estate portfolio in the Washington, D.C. metro area.[12] The financial and energy savings are significant.

Another great way to save energy use is to have buildings cleaned dur-ing the day. Not only will this reduce the lighting, air conditioning, and heat-ing used at night for the cleaning crew, but it will improve the quality of the work environment for contractors.

USE STRATEGIES TAILORED TO YOUR BUSINESS

Not every business is the same, and those that heavily rely on energy for cer-tain functions may find a relatively short-term payback through investments in new technologies or infrastructure. The United Parcel Service (UPS), for ex-ample, uses technology to help minimize the number of left turns made by the company's roughly 95,000 package delivery vehicles. The technology does this by designing delivery routes in a loop with as few left turns as possible. Not only does this minimize fuel use and emissions by reducing unnecessary idling, it is actually safer because it decreases the number of times a driver turns across oncoming traffic. The UPS managers use a combination of personal and historical experience as well as specialized, sophisticated computer programs to plan every delivery route. Last year alone, the company's use of technology and experience saved 30 million miles and 3 million gallons of fuel.[13]

Consider ways to leverage relationships with those who provide energy and water to your organization while benefiting the environment at the same time. Adobe, for example, participates in Pacific Gas and Electric's (PG&E) demand response program. On days when it's particularly hot and demand for cooling buildings goes up, PG&E can call Adobe's facilities team and they will reduce the company's use of energy by up to 10 percent if needed, both to help protect the grid and to hold down critical peak pricing. In exchange, Adobe's overall rate is lowered. Most of the energy reduction is around lighting—in interior hallways and exterior-facing offices. This initiative has particularly strong support from employees, who have been told that, on a hot day you may notice lights will be diminished to save energy and save costs." This makes employees feel that they are doing their part, and turns what might be a source of annoyance into a source of shared pride.

Waste Not, Want Not

When discussing the reduction of waste, most people refer to material waste, such as municipal solid waste or waste created from construction and demolition, mining, quarrying, and manufacturing. It also refers to reducing toxic waste and emissions that impact land, air, and water. The ideal for environmentalists (and indeed for those organizations who like to save money) is the concept of "zero waste." With zero waste, the goal is to effectively create a closed-loop industrial system in which the traditional concept of waste is eliminated. Instead of something to be removed, waste should be considered as a residual product or simply a potential resource for some other function. This involves rethinking business processes in order to eliminate hazardous properties that make waste products unusable and unmanageable in quantities that overburden both industry and the environment. William McDonough and Michael Braungart refer to this concept as Cradle to Cradle, or "waste equals food."[14]

Zero-waste strategies consider the entire life cycle of products, processes and systems in the context of a comprehensive systems understanding of interactions with nature and search for inefficiencies at all stages.

With this understanding, waste can be prevented through designs based on full life-cycle thinking. Any waste created should be "planned" waste with the potential for future applications. Ironically, humans are the only animals that create surplus waste—all other species have managed to fully adopt this zero-waste concept. But companies and cities everywhere are now taking the plunge and setting ambitious targets to do just this. Nike has made strides to engage in zero-waste product design, using recyclable polymers, water-based solvents (which reduce both toxins and energy consumption), and fabric woven from used soda bottles. Their Reuse-A-Shoe program is particularly compelling. Worn-out athletic shoes of any brand are collected, processed, and recycled into material used in sports surfaces like basketball courts, tennis courts, athletic fields, running tracks, and playgrounds for young people around the world. Since the birth of Reuse-A-Shoe in 1990, they have recycled more than 21 million pairs of athletic shoes into more than 265 sport surfaces.

Getting to zero waste is a difficult goal for many companies and individuals to achieve, but a surprising number of organizations are taking conscious steps to get there by reducing, reusing, and recycling aggressively. Here are some creative examples and approaches:

INTEGRATING WASTE STRATEGIES

Reducing use, reusing products, and recycling products are strategies embraced by many organizations because they are just good business practices and they save money. Most companies take on a combination of each of these strategies to effectively reduce costs and avoid sending waste to the landfill. For example, Anheuser-Busch effectively reduced waste by "light weighting"—reducing the amount of aluminum used to produce its twenty-four-ounce cans by 5.1 million pounds and saving 7.5 million pounds of paperboard by decreasing the thickness of its twelve-pack bottle packaging (numbers from 2003). Additionally, Anheuser-Busch maintains an expansive organic waste reuse program, using 10.3 million pounds of beechwood chips—a byproduct of the brewing process—to produce compost and mulch. The company uses the byproducts in its many theme parks, such as Sea

World and Busch Gardens. Also, Anheuser-Busch is a founding member of the Buy Recycled Business Alliance, and is one of the largest purchasers of recycled-content products in the United States.[15]

The Walt Disney Company decreased paper usage and saved $25,000 in 2000 by ordering office supplies electronically instead of by fax. Disney also saved more than $150,000 by establishing a company-wide return program for toner cartridges. In addition, the company commissary implemented a policy of using salad bar plates for dine-in meals; disposable packaging is used only for take-out orders. Walt Disney Studios also maintains a database that lists all reusable sets and props to facilitate sharing these materials, while the lighting department donates used lighting gels to the Los Angeles Children's Museum for art projects such as kaleidoscopes and imitation stained glass. The company collects recyclable materials, including plastics, wood, mixed paper, and corrugated packaging.[16]

RECYCLING WITH INCENTIVES

There are a growing number of examples of organizations and individuals making money by recycling or at least significantly reducing the cost of waste handling. For example, Norcal Waste Systems, San Francisco's trash hauler, provides customers with color-coded 32-gallon carts: a blue cart for paper, glass, plastics, and metal recycling; a green cart for food and yard waste; and a black cart that's destined for the landfill. San Franciscans get about $5 off the standard $22-a-month collection rate if they can make do with a smaller black bin, sending less to the landfill. Merchants earn discounts for recycling, and Norcal receives bonuses from local municipalities for keeping waste out of landfills.[17] Sprint sells its corporate dry and wet waste to its recycling vendor. It uses the "kickback" money it receives to fund other green workplace initiatives.[18]

E-CYCLING

Particularly in the workplace, electronic waste is a major concern. Many of the materials in our computers, phones, servers, monitors, and handheld devices have the potential to contribute significant levels of toxic materials to landfills. These include lead, polychlorinated biphenyls, mercury, cadmium, arsenic, zinc, chromium, and selenium.[19] E-cycling can be as simple as setting up a battery and cell-phone recycling box in the office to as complex as organizing a full-scale community program. Concerned organizations are taking steps to greatly reduce electronic goods in the waste stream. Apple, Dell, Hewlett Packard, Best Buy, Panasonic, and Sony have partnered with the Electronic Industries Alliance's Consumer Education Initiative and are now offering grants to help increase the recycling opportunities in local communities.[20] Apple has a particularly holistic approach to recycling, which includes extensive take-back programs that enable consumers and businesses to dispose of used Apple equipment in an environmentally sound manner. Since the first take-back initiative began in Germany in 1994, Apple has launched programs in the United States, Canada, Japan, and throughout Europe, diverting over 34 million pounds of electronic equipment from landfills worldwide. Apple's take-back program offers U.S. customers environmentally friendly recycling of their old computer when they buy a new Mac—regardless of the manufacturer.

Unusual Partnerships

After reducing the use of natural resources at the beginning (through procurement) and at the end (through waste reduction), what happens in between? Traditionally, operational strategies are about making the most of assets to generate recurring income or to increase the value of the business in some way. When it comes to green operations, the same holds true, but operations must also avoid adversely affecting the environment or the health and wellness of people. For this reason, looking beyond the organization becomes very important. Thinking through green operational strategies that only pertain to your building or your business can be very environmentally and economically beneficial, but will not have nearly the impact of enrolling other stakeholders to help you. Truly transformative green strategies that move beyond incremental environmental improvements require the organization to consider the larger context and engage in new partnerships.

THINK AT A CITY-WIDE OR REGIONAL LEVEL

Consider partnering and collaborating with government groups, non-governmental organizations, community initiatives/associations, or similar organizations to create larger solutions with greater impact. The Enwave Energy Corporation, through partial financial backing from the City of Toronto, developed the deep lake water cooling system that uses cold water to air-condition high-rise buildings in downtown Toronto. It currently cools 47 buildings and benefits the city and the tenants of each of these facilities by:

- Reducing energy consumption by up to 90 percent (compared to conventional chillers)
- Reducing carbon-dioxide emissions
- Improving the water supply by using new intake pipes that are deeper
- Investing in a corporation in which the city is a shareholder

How does this work exactly? Enwave's three intake pipes draw lake water (at 4 degrees Celsius) five kilometers off the shore of Lake Ontario, eighty-three meters below the surface. The naturally cold water makes its way to the city's John Street Pumping Station. There, heat exchangers facilitate the energy transfer between the icy cold lake water and the Enwave closed chilled water supply loop.

The water drawn from the lake continues on its regular route through the John Street Pumping Station for normal distribution into the city water supply. Enwave uses only the coldness from the lake water, not the actual water (causing minimal effects to ecology), to provide the alternative to conventional air-conditioning. At full capacity, the deep lake water cooling system will reduce mainstream electricity use by a factor equivalent to 6,800 homes, which will also prevent 79,000 tons of carbon dioxide from entering the air—a carbon dioxide savings equivalent to taking 15,800 cars off the road.[21]

CONSIDER WAYS TO SHARE THE SAME RESOURCE

BMW recently put out a request for proposal to build a warehouse in Pennsylvania. The developers who won made a deal with the automaker that proposed keeping ownership rights of the roof. They plan to build a massive solar array and then sell energy back to the grid. Additional structure was needed for the roof, but the developer could afford this (and bid competitively) based on the energy income they plan to receive.[22]

FIND NEW WAYS OF FUNDING INITIATIVES

Particularly in times of financial uncertainty, funding capital spending projects can be difficult to justify. Explore federal, state, and local grants, tax credits, or other alternative means to get your projects underway. The Intrago (pronounced Intra-Go) Corporation, together with the University of Washington and other partners, has been awarded funding from the Washington State Department of Transportation for a shared electric vehicle system at the University's Seattle campus. The funding is part of a program that fosters innovation to help reduce automobile trips into congested areas such as urban university campuses. The campus network of self-rented electric bicycles aims to reduce the number of automobile commute trips in the region. Intrago is addressing the unmet need for on-demand personal mobility that is clean, right-sized, and enjoyable to use for short-distance trips around university and corporate campuses as well as high-density urban and public transit locations. Users may select any bicycle at a station and then return it to any location on the Seattle campus.

GREENING OPERATIONS AND managing the full cycle of a company's assets can be best accomplished via a highly creative process. Yes, there are often constraints and limitations due to scarce resources, but the solutions are often only limited by imagination. And being creative does not mean making wholesale changes or taking on a great deal of risk. Changes as simple as replacing light bulbs, recycling, composting, or buying green cleaning products can make an environmental impact and help to challenge the current way of doing things.

Now that you've changed your organization's behavior, leveraged technology, and integrated green thinking into your business operations, how can you integrate green thinking into the design of your workplace? The next important step in fully integrating your green strategy is about not only designing your space with a green eye, but thinking like a designer in order to transform your business.

Actions You Can Take Today

1. Try strategies listed under Saving Energy and Water. You don't have to do everything all at once. Pick a few and work them into your daily habits.
2. Make a list of partnership organizations your company might leverage and engage. Consider local governments, energy companies, your children's school, or community organizations. Make informal contacts and seek out opportunities to join forces.
3. Reduce, reuse, and recycle.

CHAPTER 9

Transformative Design

We shall require a substantially new manner of thinking if mankind is to survive.

—Albert Einstein

By analyzing the way buildings have evolved over thousands of years, there is much to be learned from the past. Indigenous populations have always used local resources to create shelter. And the environmental impact of these structures has been almost negligible. Consider the tipi popularized by the Native Americans of the Great Plains. A tipi (also tepee, or teepee) is a durable conical tent, originally made of animal skins or birch bark that provides warmth and comfort in winter, is dry during heavy rains, and is cool in the heat of summer. Tipis could be disassembled and packed away quickly when a tribe decided to move, and could be reconstructed quickly after settling in a new area. This portability was important to those Plains Indians who had a nomadic lifestyle.

Consider also the *rondavel,* a traditional African home made of mud and straw. These structures, usually round in shape, are traditionally made with materials that can be locally obtained in raw form. The *rondavel's* walls are often constructed from stones with mortar that may consist of sand, soil, or some combination of these mixed with dung. The floor is finished with a processed dung mixture to make it smooth. The roof braces of the *rondavel* are made out of tree limbs cut to length. The roof itself is thatch sewn to the wooden braces with grass rope. The process of completing the thatch can take one weekend or up to a year if done by a skilled artisan, as it must be sewn in one section at a time, starting from the bottom working toward the top. As each section is sewn, it is weathered and aged in to form a complete weatherproof seal.

Ironically, neither the tipi nor the *rondavel* is likely to receive an architectural design award or Leadership in Energy and Environmental Design (LEED) or Building Research Establishment Environmental Assessment Method (BREEAM) certification for their design ingenuity, but they are some of the most sustainable structures in existence. Zero-waste structures are just not part of the building vocabulary in a postindustrial society. Demographic and market forces pressure designers and builders to use more materials, water, and energy to support a global economy while increasing humanity's ecological footprint. The old Native American proverb, "Take only what you need and leave the land as you found it," becomes an almost impossible target. Design alone will not be the quick fix to solving environmental problems. That said, there is much to be learned from the way designers approach problems that can help transform the way organizations solve problems, and can help spur tremendous benefits for the environment.

New Ways of Thinking

Solving environmental problems requires thinking and acting differently, because traditional approaches—to business, industry, and policy—will only take organizations down a path that is the status quo. Many claim that business as usual is what caused major environmental problems to begin with. That's where "design thinking" comes in to play. In 1969, Nobel Laureate Herbert Simon noted that "[e]ngineering, medicine, business, architecture, and painting are concerned not with the necessary but with the contingent—not with how things are, but with how they might be—in short, with design. Everyone designs who devises courses of action aimed at changing existing situations into preferred ones. Design, so construed, is the core of all professional training."[1]

Successful designers (of buildings, products, services, and organizations) must be willing to admit that there is no "set solution" and that the answer to making the planet greener cannot be bought off a shelf. Instead, environmentally savvy designers use their principles, creativity, and a willingness to learn and adapt to guide them to new and more sustainable solutions. For many organizations, this way of thinking requires new skills and a different process for developing solutions.

Think back several decades. The traditional twentieth-century company was successful because of its hierarchical structure, division of labor, clear chain of command, economies of scale, and the controls in place that kept it running efficiently. The traditional organizational model, initially based on practices established during the industrial revolution, worked well for twentieth-century business needs. Though much of these structural features are still relevant, there are some that will not be as useful in the twenty-first century, given the breakthroughs needed to differentiate business solutions and solve seemingly impossible environmental obstacles.

Roger Martin, Dean of the Rotman School of Management at the University of Toronto, asserts that modern firms should become more like design shops. He notes:

> Whereas traditional firms organize around ongoing task and permanent assignments, in design shops, work flows around projects with defined terms. The source of status in traditional firms is managing big budgets and large staffs, but in design shops it derives from building a track record of finding solutions to incredibly complex problems—solving tough mysteries with elegant solutions. Whereas the style of work in traditional firms involves defining roles and seeking the perfect answers, design firms feature extensive collaboration, "charettes" (focused brainstorming sessions) and constant dialogue with clients.[2]

Also important in any design process, in addition to intellectual curiosity and tenacity, are defining limits for the creative process and focusing on performance-based solutions that combine aesthetics, function, and long-term impacts. Solving for one of these factors is not enough. Here are a few examples of green products and services developed using the designer mentality:

THE SOLAR BOTTLE

One-sixth of the world's population has no access to safe drinking water, increasing the risk of waterborne diseases such as diarrhea, cholera, typhoid fever, Hepatitis A, and dysentery.

When attending an exhibition with the theme "H_2O" at Milan's International Furniture Fair, Alberto Meda, a furniture and lighting designer, and Francisco Gomez Paz, an industrial designer, learned about the solar water disinfection system (SODIS)—a simple, low-cost solution for treating drinking water at a household level. Transparent plastic bottles are filled with contaminated water. When exposed to full sunlight for six hours, the pathogens in the water are destroyed.

Meda and Paz designed a container that brings out the best of the SODIS system, and the result is Solar Bottle, which has one transparent face for ultraviolet A and infrared ray collection and an aluminum color to increase the reflections (see Figure 9.1). The high-ratio surface and thickness of the low-cost container improves the performance of solar disinfection, and its flat shape makes it stackable and facilitates storage. A handle makes it possible to regulate the angle for best solar exposition and ensures easy transportation.

EDIBLE UTENSILS

Seppiolino, a product in the prototype phase, is an edible fork/spoon utensil made of dough that hardens and becomes crispy. Designed by Davide Tarantino, a student in Italy, it can be personalized and flavored using food products locally available, such as wheat, corn, rice, or flour. It is industrially produced, poured into a mold and cooked. As an alternative to plastic, wood, or metal cutlery, it also helps minimize costs and materials. Besides replacing common throwaway cutlery, Seppiolino helps save energy, reduces waste, and minimizes the accumulations of nonrecyclable plastic.

ERASABLE PAPER

Xerox Corporation scientists have invented a way to make prints whose images last only a day, so that the paper can be used again and again. The tech-

Figure 9.1: The solar bottle.

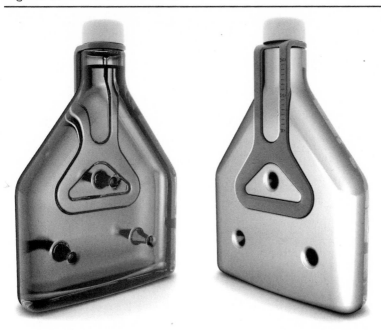

Designers: Alberto Meda and Francisco Gomez Paz   *Image*: Miro Zagnoli

nology, still in a preliminary state, blurs the line between paper documents and digital displays and could ultimately lead to a significant reduction in paper use. Xerox estimates that as many as two out of every five pages printed in the office are for what it calls "daily" use, such as e-mails, Web pages, and reference materials that have been printed for a single viewing. Since their research estimates that the 15.2 trillion pages printed worldwide will grow 30 percent over the next 10 years,[3] the use of erasable paper could have a significant positive environmental impact.

The solar bottle, edible utensils, and erasable paper are examples of products whose creators took complex problems and created new and viable solutions through intense research, creativity, and an understanding of unique issues. But what is it about "design thinking" (a term referring to a more creative process for solving problems or issues) that is so different from other approaches to solving problems? Jeanne Liedtka, with the University of Virginia's Darden Graduate School of Business, teaches design innovation to business students. In her work *Strategy as Design,* she describes design thinking as strategic and necessary for business success because it has the following attributes[4]:

- *Synthetic.* Design thinking includes the weaving together or synthesis of often-disparate demands, which frequently change over the course of trying to understand a given problem. This process of integrating multiple and ever-changing constraints will often achieve results and solutions that are successful because they consider many factors at the same time.

- *Abductive.* Inductive thinking—taking specific instances to create a general theory—and deductive thinking—using the general theory to predict specific instances—work well in science for proving things that already exist. Design thinking, however, is abductive in nature, or primarily concerned with the process of visualizing what might be (some desired future state) and then creating a blueprint for realizing that vision.

- *Hypothesis-driven.* Design is largely hypothesis-driven in that it involves making assumptions about cause-and-effect relationships. Based on previous behaviors, designers make assumptions that are then tested and evaluated.

- *Opportunistic.* The thrill of design work is in looking for new possibilities and chances to test more and more complex issues and problems as they arise.

- *Dialectical.* The process of design is a balance between requirements and possibilities. It is a tug of war between cost, budget, and schedule on one side, and exploration and creativity on the other.

- *Inquiring and value-driven.* Design thinking is open to scrutiny and willing to make its reasoning explicit to a broader audience. It recognizes that value judgments are being made and uses these values to connect rather than to alienate. Communication is critical to sharing and testing these values. Even in training, designers open themselves up to scrutiny by their professors and by visiting professionals. Good design firms continue this practice of critique at all stages of product or service development.

Designers use a combination of these approaches to define and solve problems. Design thinking is particularly relevant for solving complex environmental problems that require cross-disciplinary, integrated solutions. The results are often not one, but a series of innovative and creative solutions, some of which work more successfully than others. Sometimes even the process of designing is a learning tool in itself.

How is design thinking transforming the way you design your green workplaces? And how can it help to green your business? Consider ways design thinking can help solve the environmental problems described in this book: reducing your ecological footprint (energy, water, and raw material use); escaping our addiction to oil; reducing waste and emissions; and improving indoor air quality.

Transformative Design in Buildings

Transformative building design questions conventional thinking toward reducing environmental impact. It uses design thinking to go from making incremental changes to taking giant innovative leaps. It solves multiple problems and integrates human behavior, technology, operations, and design. As an example, consider the problem of water. In urban environments, water typically comes from the municipal water supply, which collects water from rivers, lakes, or underground aquifers. It is then treated and distributed through a sophisticated system of ducts and pumps into commercial and residential buildings. Once there, it's used in sinks, lavatories, landscaping, and cleaning processes. Most of the water used for all of these functions is the highest quality available, i.e., "potable," or appropriate for human consumption. After use, this "dirty" water (either "gray water" from dishwashing, laundry, or bathing, or "black water" from toilets) is typically dumped into lakes and streams also used for recreation. Because there is only a limited amount of fresh water in the world and our requirements for water are increasing, dumping dirty water into lakes and streams only exacerbates the problem.

Many organizations have recognized this and have developed better practices to collect, use, and dispose of their water in a more environmentally friendly way. They are reducing the total water they use, their consumption of potable water, and the amount of storm water that runs off their facilities and parking lots into waterways (water that runs off parking lots contains oil and other contaminants from vehicles toxic to the environment). Examples of strategies to decrease water use include no- or low-flow fixtures, such as sinks or toilets, automatic water shut-off fixtures, and growing native plants that do not require supplemental irrigation. Design strategies that reduce the need for potable water include using water captured from the roof (gray water) for toilet flushing or landscape irrigation. Design strategies that reduce polluted storm water run-off include using green roofs and bioswales (landscape elements designed to remove silt and pollution from surface runoff water). In addition to reducing gray or black water going into lakes and streams, these strategies are quickly becoming a requirement for development in many cities.

These practices are excellent ways to reduce the water use in your building or minimize the impact of storm water runoff from parking lots, but really *transformative* strategies minimize the need for using municipal water at all. How so? They capture rain water, make it potable, use it in the building, and then clean it again. These strategies help buildings become self-sustaining because they capture and reuse what they need while minimizing water sent to rivers, lakes, and other waterways. Two examples of particularly innovative water systems are living walls and Living Machines:

- Living walls are made up of pre-vegetated panels or fabric systems that are attached to structural walls or frames as a means of water reuse as well as thermal insulation. The plants purify slightly polluted water (such as gray water) by digesting the dissolved nutrients. Bacteria mineralize the organic components to make them available to plants. Living walls are particularly suitable for cities, as they allow good use of available vertical surface areas. They are sometimes built indoors to improve indoor air quality, minimizing "sick building syndrome."
- Living Machines are a form of biological wastewater treatment designed to mimic the cleansing functions of wetlands. They are artificial intensive bioremediation systems including aquatic and wetland plants, bacteria, algae, protozoa, plankton, snails, clams, fish, and other organisms to provide specific cleansing functions.

BEYOND WATER, WHAT are other examples of transformative design related to helping the environment? The very best and most interesting tend to be strategies that solve many business and environmental problems at the same time. Here are two particularly transformative design ideas that are beginning to take root.

VERTICAL FARMS

The concept of vertical farms was created in 1999 by Dr. Dickson Despommier with Columbia University graduate students in his class on medical ecology (the study of how the environment and human health interact). The vertical farm proposes integrating agriculture into urban high-rises. Using greenhouse methods and recycled resources, these buildings would produce fruit, vegetables, fish, and livestock year-round in cities. Proposals and competitions for designing vertical farms are happening from New York to Seattle to Toronto to Las Vegas. Though there is an increase in upfront and operating costs, there seem to be limitless benefits to the idea:

- Year-round crop production is possible, allowing one indoor acre to be the equivalent of four to six outdoor acres or more, depending upon the crop (e.g., when growing strawberries, one indoor acre is the equivalent of thirty outdoor acres of land)
- No weather-related crop failures due to droughts, floods, or pests
- Agricultural runoff is virtually eliminated by recycling black water
- Farmland is returned to nature, restoring ecosystem functions and services
- Reduced incidence of many infectious diseases that are acquired at the agricultural interface
- Decreased fossil fuel use (no tractors or plows needed)[5]

BIOMIMICRY

Biomimicry (from *bios*, meaning life, and *mimesis*, meaning to imitate) is a relatively new science that studies the models, systems, processes, and elements of nature, and then imitates or takes creative inspiration from them to solve human problems sustainably. In her 1997 book, *Biomimicry: Innovation Inspired by Nature*, Janine M. Benyus introduces the concept: "Our planet-mates (plants, animals and microbes) have been patiently perfecting their wares for more than 3.8 billion years . . . turning rock and sea into a life-friendly home. What better models could there be?"[6] Here are a couple of outcomes of this brilliant and transformative design process:

- *Self-cleaning surfaces.* Ask any schoolchild or adult how leaves keep water from sticking to them, and they'll almost certainly say, "Because they are so smooth." Yet one of the most water-repellent leaves in the world, that of the lotus, isn't smooth at all. The myriad crevices of its microscopically rough leaf surface trap a maze of air upon which water droplets float, so that the slightest breeze or tilt in the leaf causes balls of water to roll cleanly off, taking attached dirt particles with them. Now, microscopically rough surface additives have been introduced into a new generation of paint, glass, and fabric finishes, greatly reducing the need for chemical or laborious cleaning. For example, GreenShield, a fabric finish made by G3i based on the "lotus effect," achieves the same water and stain repellency as conventional fabric finishes while using eight times less harmful fluorinated chemicals.

- *Natural air conditioning.* Most people think of termites as destroying buildings, not helping design them. But the Eastgate Building, an office complex in Harare, Zimbabwe, has an air conditioning system modeled on the self-cooling mounds of *macrotermes michaelseni* (termites). Termites in Zimbabwe build gigantic mounds inside of which they farm a fungus that is their primary food source. The fungus must be kept at exactly 87 degrees Fahrenheit, while the temperatures outside range from 35 degrees Fahrenheit at night to 104 degrees Fahrenheit during the day. The termites achieve this remarkable feat by constantly opening and closing a series of heating and cooling vents throughout the mound over the course of the day. With a system of carefully adjusted convection currents, air is sucked in at the lower part of the mound, down into enclosures with muddy walls, and up through a channel to the peak of the termite mound. The industrious termites constantly dig new vents and plug up old ones in order to regulate the temperature.

  Architect Mick Pearce collaborated with engineers at Arup Associates to design the Eastgate Centre, which uses 90 percent less energy for ventilation than conventional buildings its size, and has already saved the building owners over \$3.5 million in air conditioning costs. The Eastgate Centre, largely made of concrete, has a ventilation system that operates in a similar way. Outside air that is drawn in is either warmed or cooled by the building mass depending on which is hotter, the building concrete or the air. It is then vented into the building's floors and offices before exiting through chimneys at the top.

Transformative building design—especially that which is inspired by the environment—is abductive, exploratory, collaborative, and multi-disciplinary. It takes science, technology, art, economics, and natural systems into account and produces varied yet highly sophisticated solutions. It also sets limits on the use of natural resources to question the essence of the problem we are trying to solve.

Design Influencing Green Behavior

Transformative design is at its best when it not only changes the way products and services are made and delivered, but also increases consumer awareness and changes human behavior at the same time. In many cases, the very act of using a green product or service creates an either conscious or subconscious reaction in the user. To influence sustainable behavior, especially through design, it is important to inform users in a transparent way about the right decision to make, to put them in control of their decision, and to let them know their actions count toward a larger social good.[7]

Some clever examples of services and products that influence behavior in the marketplace include:

THE \$100 LAPTOP

One Laptop per Child was set up by faculty members at the Massachusetts Institute of Technology (MIT) Media Lab to create the "\$100 laptop." Their goal was to provide personal computer access to children all over the world, particularly to children in developing countries with poor infrastructure or a lack of reliable electricity. The laptops are wireless, and were powered by a hand crank (the hand crank caused concerns about stresses on the casing and ease of use, so now they are powered by bicycle instead). The social impact of the laptop is substantial, as it has the potential to serve the nearly two billion children in the developing world who are inadequately educated or receive no education at all. The laptop is also available for children (or adults) in the developed world. But because the computer is manually powered, there is a direct correlation between the effort required to power it and the power it needs, optimizing efficiency. There are many other electronics that work in the same way—hand-crank powered light-emitting diode (LED) flashlights, rechargers, radios, and the like.

KEEP THE CHANGE

In 2004, Bank of America (BofA) hired IDEO, a design consultancy based in Palo Alto, California, to help conceive of and conduct ethnographic research on baby boomer–age women with children. The goal was to discover how to get this consumer segment to open new checking and savings accounts. For the next several months, a team of BofA and IDEO researchers visited Atlanta, Baltimore, and San Francisco. They observed a dozen families and interviewed people on the streets. They watched people at home as they paid and balanced their checkbooks. They tagged along with mothers as they shopped, dined, and made deposits at drive-through ATMs. The team came to two realizations: (1) people often "rounded up" their financial transactions when writing checks because it was more convenient; and (2) many boomer women with children did not save. Instead, they used their "would-be" savings for everyday life, their children, or the household. From this research, BofA started their Keep the Change program. Every time a customer buys something with his or her Bank of America Check Card, BofA rounds up the purchase to the nearest dollar amount and transfers the difference to that customer's checking or savings account. Since the launch, 2.5 million customers have signed up for Keep the Change. Over seven hundred thousand have opened new checking accounts and one million people have signed on for new savings accounts. This is good news for BofA and good for the many women who are increasing their personal wealth through this product.

BUILDINGS THAT TEACH

It costs $200,000 for a full-page advertisement in the *Wall Street Journal,* a page that is probably only looked at for five seconds. But the buildings you sit in every day have an incredible amount of "advertising space" on walls, windows, roofs, ceilings, and floors at a significantly lower cost per square inch. Think of your office not as a finished product, but as a billboard and a laboratory for testing green strategies and innovations. If employees can see ideas at work in the office, they will learn something new and are more likely to try them at home. Sidwell Friends Middle School in Washington, D.C. has taken this to heart by engaging students, parents, and the community in the design and construction of their Leadership in Energy and Environmental Design (LEED) Platinum facility. Here are just a few of the many green strategies that provide ongoing teaching opportunities in their building:

- Green roof and photovoltaic panels on the roof and weather station
- On-site constructed wetland that treats all water used on site and recycles it for reuse in the building's toilets, urinals, and cooling towers
- A building "skin" constructed of recycled wine and grape juice casks
- Exterior light shelves that reduce heat gain/cooling load and glare and interior light shelves that reflect daylight into classrooms, minimizing the need for artificial light
- Solar chimneys on the roof for improved natural ventilation
- Native and adaptive landscaping that reduces the need for insecticides and irrigation
- Carbon-dioxide monitors in public areas that trigger the building's mechanical system to increase fresh air when room occupancy increases
- Occupancy sensors in each room that turn off the lights when there is no movement and photo sensors throughout the building that measure available natural light and dim electric lights as required to reduce energy consumption.

To reinforce its message of using the building as a learning tool, Sidwell maintains an online, real-time dashboard of its electricity use, water reuse, and weather conditions (http://buildingdashboard.com/clients/sidwell/). The school uses its facility to not only teach students, but also the community, offering regular tours to architects, public officials and other community groups (www.sidwell.edu/green_tour/).

EACH OF THESE examples encourages greener behavior through brilliant design thinking and informs users in a transparent way of the social or environmental impact of their decisions. But when it comes to the workplace, design must address not just environmentally and socially conscious behavior, but productive behavior. After all, employee efficiency and effectiveness is a critical driver for business success.

Designing a Productive, Green Workplace

If designed and managed well, a green workplace can be highly productive and contribute directly to the bottom line. But how do you define productivity? Human productivity in the workplace typically refers to the amount of output per unit of input (labor, equipment, and capital) and can be measured in a number of ways. In a factory, productivity might be measured based on the number of hours it takes to produce a good, while in the service sector, productivity might be measured by sales generated per employee.

Measuring productivity, particularly as it relates to the workplace or a physical setting, has taken some time to understand with regard to knowledge work. Many workers are on the move and the nature of their work varies day to day. That said, across the board, people require consistent attributes in their workplace in order to be at their productive best. Environments that support rather than disrupt human productivity have a competitive advantage over those that do not. Not surprisingly, there are several factors involved with creating spaces that support workers' ability to be effective and efficient on the job.

PRODUCTIVITY ENHANCERS

Physical attributes that have been linked to productive work environments include a connection to nature, ability to exercise, sensory change and variability, personal control of environment, and good indoor air quality.

Productivity inhibitors include noise and visual distractions as well as interruptions. There is a strong connection between elements of green spaces and spaces that support human productivity.

- *Connection to nature.* Humans have a strong desire to connect to nature. This hypothesis, known as "Biophilia" and introduced and popularized by E. O. Wilson, suggests that there is an instinctive bond between human beings and other living systems. In *Biophilic Design: Theory, Science and Practice,* the authors describe the importance of nature for human productivity: "Nature is rife with sensory richness and variety in patterns, textures, light, and colors. All organisms respond with genetically programmed reflexes to the diurnal and seasonal patterns of sunlight and climate."[8]

  Workplaces that promote human alertness and engagement evoke qualities of nature through the use of light, air, materials, color, spatial definition, movement patterns, openings and enclosures, and connections to the outdoors. "Nature" in this case specifically refers to daylight, views of outdoor natural spaces, views of the sky and weather, water features, gardens, interior plantings, outdoor plazas, or interior atria with daylight and vegetation, and natural materials and décor.[9]

  Humans are hard-wired to enjoy landscapes and natural elements. In two studies of office workers, Lisa Heschong, an architect and researcher specializing in the impacts of day lighting on human performance, found that those with full window views, especially views of nature, performed better on a number of work tasks. [10] One of the studies, conducted in a call center, found that workers with seated window views performed 6 to 7 percent faster (were able to handle more calls) than those without window views. This savings does not seem significant until you multiply ten thousand call center workers by their salary. Over the course of a year, this could mean a $10 to 20 million annual productivity increase. In Heschong's second study, a field experiment, she found a positive correlation between window views and computerized memory and attention tasks. Furthermore, the quality of the view mattered.

Those with full, high-quality views with natural vegetation performed 10 to 25 percent better on these tasks than those with a limited or artificial view.

- *Ability to exercise.* An increasing number of public health officials are
  looking at how the physical environment can reduce obesity and improve physiological functioning through stair climbing and increased
  walking between buildings. The design of a building can facilitate exercise through open interior stairways, attractive outdoor walking
  paths, in-house exercise facilities, and skip-floor elevators to encourage stair climbing.[11] Providing access to exercise not only helps stimulate creativity and focus, but also decreases sick days and reduces
  corporate health-care costs in the long run.
- *Sensory change and variability.* Acres of neutral-colored workstations,
  all with the same height and texture, as a rule, do not support human
  productivity. A lack of visual stimulation during the day can dull the
  senses and affect a worker's ability to stay alert. Specifically, stimulation should not include bright lights and noise, but rather, access to
  daylight, window views to the outdoors, materials selected with sensory experience in mind (touch, visual change, color, pleasant sounds
  and odors), spatial variability, change in lighting levels and use of highlights, and moderate levels of visual complexity.[12] When the work environment is not stimulating, employees lose focus and creative drive.
  An environment devoid of sensory stimulation and variability can lead
  to boredom and passivity.[13]

Glatting Jackson Kercher Anglin, Inc. is a planning, landscape,
and urban design firm that recently moved into a refurbished historic
building in the heart of downtown Orlando. The company designs
sustainable communities for a living and is committed to practicing
what it preaches in its new workspace. The company's building is
filled with plants and natural light and uses existing building materials whenever possible. The result is a warm mix of timber, glass, steel,
concrete, carpet, and leather that provides a stimulating environment,
encouraging movement and collaborations (see Figures 9.2 and 9.3).
In addition, the company installed showers and changing rooms to
encourage employees to bike or walk to work. In fact, more than 40

Figure 9.2: Glatting's office interior promotes exercise through its simple circulation, prominent staircase and bike racks.

Figure 9.3: Glatting's workspaces are filled with plants and natural daylight and use existing building materials whenever possible.

percent of Glatting employees walk, bike, and ride public transit instead of driving cars to the office. The company supports its employees leaving their cars at home by declining to provide free parking for employees, but paying 100 percent of the cost of transit passes, and providing secure parking for bicycles and scooters.

- *Personal control.* How many space heaters and fans are hiding under desks in your office, causing countless fire code violations? Have you ever had a situation where the thermostat switches on the wall have been turned off due to the large number of hot or cold complaints? This keeps the facility department's phone from ringing, but leads to frustration that makes everybody miserable! It turns out that each person has a slightly different idea of thermal comfort, and to keep us all at our productive best, individual control of the environment is important. But it's not just temperature and air flow—productivity increases with individual control over noise, lighting, desk height, monitor color, keyboard button location, and chair adjustability. One research study tracked workers in an insurance company as they moved to a new building with advanced thermal controls in their workstations.[14] The study found that productivity increases of 2.8 percent could be attributed to the new workstations.[15]

- *Indoor Air Quality.* Sick building syndrome is the common name given to the negative effects of poor air quality in the workplace. Table 9.1, provided by the American Society of Heating, Refrigeration and Air-conditioning Engineers,[16] gives an overview of some of the worst ailments caused by buildings. Preventing these can primarily be accomplished through strict use of green cleaning procedures, heating, ventilation, and air conditioning (HVAC) system maintenance, the selection of green materials and furniture systems, improved outside air ventilation, proper construction sequencing, and proper building envelope design.

Productivity inhibitors

In an effort to create spaces with more natural light (and to increase collaboration), green workplaces are often designed to be more "open" with fewer enclosed offices. But all of this open space has not come without some neg-

Table 9.1   Ailments Caused in the Workplace

Ailments	Cause in the Workplace
Rhinitis sinusitis	Molds, laser toner, carbonless copy paper, cleaning agents
Asthma	Molds, laser toner, carbonless copy paper, cleaning agents
Hypersensitivity pneumonitis	Molds, moisture
Organic dust toxic syndrome	Gram-negative[17] bacteria
Contact dermatitis	Molds, laser toner, carbonless copy paper
Contact urticaria	Office products, carbonless copy paper
Eye irritation	Low relative humidity, volatile organic compounds, particulates
Nasal irritation	Low relative humidity, volatile organic compounds, particulates
Central nervous system symptoms	Volatile organic compounds, carbon monoxide, cytokines from bioaerosol exposure
Legionnaires' disease	Aerosols from contaminated water sources, shower heads, water faucet aerators, humidifiers, potable water sources (hot water heaters)

ative effects. The most common are acoustic and visual distractions, glare, and interruptions.

- *Acoustic and visual distractions.* Open-office environments (work settings that have few enclosed offices with full-height walls) are quickly becoming more common than enclosed environments. Open offices are generally considered more "green" in that they require less artificial light, material use, and ventilation. Enclosed offices require walls that are often torn down or moved many times over the life of the building. This causes material waste, dust, and general disruption to employees. Enclosed offices also tend to block natural light to other areas of the floor, particularly when they are located along the perimeter wall. In an open office environment, people can see and hear each other more often and they are more likely to communicate. This can be a good thing for organizational effectiveness, but can hinder productivity, particularly when employees are trying to do tasks that require a high degree of concentration. Interestingly, when employees have some degree of self-control over the noise in their environment, they are less distracted by it.[18]

Research on open offices shows that visual distractions associated with the continual movement of people has created high levels of dissatisfaction. This has lead to the widespread use of partitioned workstations (cubicles). Although partitions reduce visual distractions, they have not adequately reduced the noise distractions described above.[19] The solution for many organizations is to provide a mix of workspaces for their employees to move around in during the day, some of which have acoustic and visual privacy. Other organizations have invested in sound masking (white noise) or have built smaller open areas (not just a "sea of cubes") in order to minimize noise disruption.

- *Glare.* The recent thrust for more windows and increased natural light has led to an increase in glare on computer monitors. It turns out that sometimes natural light is not a good thing when it comes to workplace productivity. This problem can be avoided through building orientation, window treatments, and other design tactics.

- *Interruptions.* Depending on the nature of the task being done, interruptions (or continuous distractions, like music or television) can increase or decrease productivity. Interruptions during simple, mundane tasks can be just the stimulation needed to keep going. Interruptions during complex work, however, require a longer period of time to re-orient, and continued interruptions are likely to have negative effects on mood that reduce the motivation to resume work.[20] Headphones are a simple solution to this problem. Also, having access to a variety of spaces to do work can help workers avoid distractions and improve their effectiveness.

For those of you reading this and thinking, "I'm not sitting by a window in my office. Does that mean I'm not productive?" Of course not. People are incredibly adaptable and are able to work productively in environments of all shapes and sizes including offices, restaurants, hotels, airplanes, and at home. Smart green workplaces take advantage of all the factors that help employees perform well wherever they happen to be. And in most cases, making your workplace green does not mean construction or moving into a new building—it's about making smart changes or investments in what you already have. Even if you are not moving to a new facility, think about how design and design thinking can affect the way you produce services or products and how simple design solutions can be integrated into your workplace.

Of course the ultimate way of applying design thinking to the workplace is to consider transformative ways to accommodate work itself. For example, does the environment that supports our most productive work need to look and act like the offices, laboratories, and factories of today? Or are they relics of the past, soon to give way to new models and paradigms altogether?

Actions You Can Take Today

1. Use design thinking to develop new business products or services.
2. Get great ideas on ways to green your workplace (and how to apply design thinking) from other designers. Try some of these places to start:

   - The Biomimicry Guild: www.biomimicryguild.com
   - Index Award: www.indexaward.dk
   - World Changing: www.worldchanging.com
   - Treehugger: www.treehugger.com
   - Inhabitat: www.inhabitat.com
   - Dezeen: www.dezeen.com
   - Dezigner: www.dezigner.com/architecture/news.html

3. To increase productivity:

   - Increase natural light and decrease artificial light. Better yet, go outside every once in a while.
   - Exercise for short periods throughout the day. Get up and stretch your legs.
   - Create spaces with sensory change and variability. Use color, artwork, or plants to liven up your work space.
   - Make adjustments to your personal workspace to support your body and work function.
   - Improve indoor air quality with plants and clean your workspace regularly with green cleaning equipment and products.
   - Decrease visual, acoustical, and glare distractions if possible.

CHAPTER 10

Changing When, Where, and How You Work

Balance is not better time management, but better boundary management. Balance means making choices and enjoying those choices.

—Betsy Jacobson, Change Management Consultant
and Executive Coach

Many workplace and business experts claim that the office of the not-so-distant future will be radically different from the office of today. Worker mobility, pressure to save natural resources and costs, and cultural shifts in how and where work happens are already starting to redefine the workplace, particularly for knowledge workers.[1] Even the most "traditional" organizations are beginning to test the boundaries of what is normal or mainstream. As of July 2007, the State of Utah, for example, moved to a four-day work week in order to recruit employees to work for the government and to save energy costs. Over seventeen thousand out of twenty-four thousand executive-branch employees in the state are now working ten-hour days Monday through Thursday. Governor Jon Huntsman admits that his state had logistics to work through in its first year of implementation (including extended daycare and other services for employees), but he says that, after close scrutiny, the benefits far outweigh the drawbacks:

- State government buildings in Utah will reduce energy consumption by 20 percent.
- The state is more likely to recruit smart, young people looking for work–life balance jobs.
- The state is more likely to retain staff—it is perceived as a "bonus" by most of their current employees to have three-day weekends all year.
- The state will be able to provide better service to its constituents with offices that are open earlier and close later Monday through Thursday, so they are better able to support citizens who work 9 a.m. to 5 p.m.[2]

How can this be? How is it that a government organization can take on such dramatic changes? What is it about the way companies do business today that allows for these major shifts in thinking?

The Shift

The traditional view of the office is that it is a physical container for all work. *Everything* work-related happens there. Boundaries and hierarchies in an organization were often reflected in the physical environment. Senior management was given the big corner offices with windows, establishing their power and rank in the organization, and employees were assigned office size based on title, status, or tenure. Though many organizations still use this model, a growing number realize that there are issues with methodology because it is based not on the work being done but on an organizational reporting structure. The high-performance workplace for knowledge workers of today is designed to loosen up the organizational boundaries to allow collaborative as well as individual work. Also, the physical environment is able to accommodate work in not just one location, but in multiple open and enclosed environments. It's about flexibility, mobility, and teamwork, all enabled by technology.

To keep up with the changes in the way people work, the workplace must evolve. As organizations realize this, a number of common trends have

Figure 10.1: Kinetix Autodesk's multi-media division
            headquarters in San Francisco shows a new take
            on the "cubicle."

Nick Merrick © Hedrich Blessing

emerged that are allowing for greener design, technology, policies, and behaviors.

Shift of emphasis from individual workspaces to a variety of collaborative areas

In the past, office spaces were primarily made up of individually assigned offices and workstations (taking up 80–90 percent of the total floor area). Now
the ratio of individually assigned spaces to shared spaces is shifting, and the
amount of individually assigned space is shrinking to 50 to 60 percent of the
floor area, with the remaining space made up of shared spaces like cafés, conference rooms, project rooms, "huddle rooms" (rooms for small groups to
have impromptu discussions), telephone rooms, and the like.

This shift to more shared or collaborative space reflects an increase in the
amount of collaboration that takes place in the office and the recognition that
this collaboration adds value. Assessing the right mix of shared spaces requires a study of the function of individuals and groups, but in general, for
knowledge workers, the more diverse the mix of spaces, the better (see Figure 10.1). This has a great deal to do with the need for flexibility to support

organizational change and personal choice. For example, for the same task, some individuals may prefer enclosed rooms or a "cone of silence" for working while others prefer to sit in a café atmosphere while listening to music. All employees can benefit from a choice to move around their office throughout the day, picking physical settings that will suit their need at any given time.

WORK FUNCTION IS OFTEN MISALIGNED WITH SPACE ALLOCATION

Many managers are assigned large enclosed offices and rarely occupy them. They are off doing their job—networking, selling, mentoring—while leaving a large, expensive vacant space behind. Their empty offices are heated and cooled, which is an operational cost to the organization and not a particularly environmentally friendly or efficient strategy for space occupancy. This often occurs because space has been assigned based on entitlement rather than job function or need. Green workspaces support function first in order to maximize space utilization.

PEOPLE ARE NOT AT THEIR DESK AS MUCH AS THEY THINK THEY ARE

Most employees think they are sitting at their desks for a majority of their day, but this is highly unlikely. Study after study shows that knowledge workers today are on the move. Take a walk through your office and look carefully at how many people are actually sitting at their desks at any one time. Very often, employees are meeting with clients, collaborating with their team in another room, working from home, or sending messages from a hand-held device from anywhere they happen to be. It's not that they are not working; it's that members of the workforce are not sitting in one place to get their job done. In fact, workplace observation studies show that, on average, people are at their desk only 40–50 percent of the time (at peak periods) and away from their desks the rest of their day.

Kevin Kelly, a Senior Architect with the U.S. General Services Administration's Work Space Delivery Program, has collected evidence through dozens of pilot workplace projects. He claims that workers across a range of organizations and throughout the country have an inaccurate sense of how they are using space. For instance, while one group may think that they are sitting at their computers 80 percent of their work day, they may be observed to be at their computers as little as 30 percent of the time! When organizations actually observe the way space is used, it can be a wake-up call and a signal to reconsider how the space *should* be designed and used to support knowledge workers.[3]

Enabled by technology and driven by shifts in the way business is done today, knowledge workers are already effective at working in many different environments in a given day. Successful workplaces support people working in multiple settings, both on- and off-site. Organizations that have adopted a more flexible work environment and a more flexible work program along with it are able to reduce their real estate, which saves costs and lowers their environmental impact.

VIRTUAL SPACE IS JUST AS IMPORTANT AS PHYSICAL SPACE

Remember back when there were no cell phones, no BlackBerrys, no Internet, and no e-mail? It's hard to imagine given the amount of work that gets done virtually today. In fact, as a whole, knowledge workers now spend more time collaborating virtually than collaborating face-to-face. Virtual space requires as much attention as physical space to support work effectiveness. It requires attention to software, hardware, lighting, ergonomics, electronic file storage, remote access, and security issues. It also means that organizations have the ability to reduce commuting and corporate travel, which allows for significant reductions in carbon footprint.

YOUR GENERATION AFFECTS YOUR PERCEPTIONS ABOUT THE WORKPLACE

There are currently four unique generations in the workplace at the same time. A great deal of study has gone into understanding the implications of this. "Generations at Work" by Ron Zemke, Claire Raines, and Bob Filipczak (2000)[4] and other sources cite research that has demonstrated how each generation has a different worldview based on events that occurred during their formative years that impact their outlook, work ethic, views of authority, leadership, relationships, and turn-offs. These generations, referred to generally as the Veterans, Baby Boomers, Generation X-ers, and the Millennials (or Generation Y-ers) have unique views about life, work, and attitudes toward each other. What this means for the work and the workplace is that there are many opinions about the most effective management, space, and tools to get work done. There are clear generational differences and preferences when it comes to using technology, the process for allocating space, and what the workspace should reflect. Flexibility and choice are important elements in the workplace for meeting the expectations of all generations.

What Is Alternative Work?

Alternative work solutions are nontraditional work arrangements that affect either work schedule or office location. Scheduling strategies include staggered shift work or flex time. Location strategies include a balance of on- and off-site work, and include shared offices, hoteling (reservable work space), satellite office, home office, or virtual office.

The major cultural shift that enables alternative work is moving away from assigning individual offices and workstations to specific people, and instead assigning space to a team, department, or mix of organizations. Alternative work environments typically provide a network of places and choices to support the business being done, which in turn increases speed to market, allows for "growth without growth" (organizational growth without increasing real estate holdings), and increases an organization's ability to respond quickly to changes in business strategy. Alternative workplaces provide settings for work wherever it happens. For example, some employees may work more effectively or efficiently in a team space, a customer location, the airport, or a hotel. Providing varied and more flexible spaces, virtual technology, and better collaboration protocols may support their work better than the traditional office. These strategies are less about dedicating offices to individuals in a one-to-one ratio and more about providing the right workplace setting at the right time and in the right place given the way employees actually work.

Many employees are resistant to the idea of not being assigned a permanent office or workstation, despite the environmental and productivity benefits. Judith Heerwagen, environmental and evolutionary psychologist, emphasizes that:

Western cultures are currently stuck on the policy of assigning every person in the office their own workplace, which is really unsustainable. Half of all workspaces are always empty, and this is a tremendous waste of resources. The current workforce is really resistant to it—including workers of all ages—even young people want their own workspace. There is a psychology behind desiring "my own space" in the sense that people want to know what to expect. But we need to move in the direction of sharing space in different ways.[5]

The implementation of new workplace strategies involves the full participation of users in developing alternative concepts with strong support by management. This approach requires a willingness to evaluate, question, and change existing work processes and resources. If implemented correctly, adopting alternative workplace strategies will allow employees to achieve their maximum productivity as well as increased efficiency, more flexible layouts, and reduced space requirements.

Table 10.1 lists typical on- and off-site options for employees that are currently being used by a number of organizations. All of them require some sort of policy to describe the rules around their use and are not necessarily viable for every employee. And all of these options, especially the satellite and remote tele-center, entail situations where the organization will need to plan ahead to accommodate the space and technology requirements of the employee prior to using them. For example, the home-office employee may need some assistance in accessing local area networks or ordering ergonomic desk furniture.

Keys to success in providing supportive on-premises workplace options:

- *Provide consistent technology infrastructure and equipment that is easily upgraded.* Provide training for use. Even if you are moving into a new office that looks exactly like your old one, it takes some time to set up and work out the kinks. In environments where employees are moving around regularly, it's worth investing in consistent provision of docking stations, laptops, phones, and wireless access so that "plug and play" is easier for employees and this doesn't tax the Facilities and Information Technology (IT) departments.
- *Establish and enforce robust protocols guiding the use of space.* Many alternative office spaces are shared by more than one employee and

Table 10.1   Alternative Work Strategies

	Strategy	Benefits	Disadvantages
Shared address	Two or more employees sharing a single, assigned workspace (such as an office or workstation)	Better space utilization Increase headcount without increasing space required	Requires timing coordination of resource use Takes away the potential to personalize space
Group address	Designated group or team space (such as a war room or project room) with walls for permanently displaying team-generated ideas for a specified period of time	Better space utilization Increase headcount without increasing space required	Requires timing coordination of resource use Takes away the potential to personalize space
Activity settings	Variety of work settings (such as a group of offices, meeting rooms, and equipment areas) to fit diverse individual or group activities	Provides users with a choice of settings *(to best respond to tasks)* Fosters team interaction	Unassigned nature of settings may result in conflicts with cultural expectations
Free address	Workspaces (such as offices, meeting rooms, or team areas) shared on a first-come, first-serve basis	Maximizes use of unassigned space Minimizes real estate overhead Minimizes cost of construction and ongoing expenses because there are more employees than seats provided Suitable for highly mobile/transient occupancies	Non-ownership takes away the potential for personalization May be inadequate accommodations on peak days in the office Requires cultural change Employees must abide by new set of protocols

(continues)

Table 10.1 (continued)

	Strategy	Benefits	Disadvantages
Hoteling	Employees call ahead to reserve workspace (typically an office or meeting room) in an office facility where there are fewer offices than employees	Accommodates staff increases without corresponding increases in facilities and leasing costs Minimizes cost of construction and ongoing expenses because there are more employees than seats provided	Reservation systems can be cumbersome–employees reserve, then don't show Effort required to keep employees from effectively "moving in" Requires cultural change Employees must abide by new protocols
Satellite office	Full-service alternate office environment, conveniently located Can be shared with other organizations to save costs	Provide "full service" accommodations in locations convenient to homes or customer locations Helps employee balance work/life Major attraction/ retention leverage	Implies less structured supervision Technology issues of phone roll-over, secure connectivity at the right speed Sizing the facility is a difficult task
Remote telecenter	Office drop-in center located away from main office, closer to clients Can be shared with other organizations to save costs	Similar benefits to satellite center, but generally only for drop-ins Allows quicker customer response Major attraction/ retention leverage	Technology issues of phone roll-over, secure connectivity at the right speed Sizing the facility is a difficult task Fewer amenities than at main site

(continues)

Table 10.1   (continued)

	Strategy	Benefits	Disadvantages
Remote telecenter (continued)		Potential reduction of space required in office locations	
Home office	Support connectivity and an appropriate working environment in the home	Helps employee balance work/life Major attraction/ retention leverage Reduces space required in office locations	Requires employee to structure time and work differently Implies alternate management/ supervision techniques
Virtual office	Work anywhere, anytime	Helps employee balance work/life Major attraction/ retention leverage Reduces space required in office locations	Seamless connectivity is a requirement Requires employee to structure time and work differently Implies alternate management/ supervision techniques

not everyone is used to sharing. Rules about desk cleanliness and no use of speaker phones in the open environment are crucial to maximizing the use of these spaces.

- *Monitor the use and condition of unassigned work areas.* When spaces are unassigned to individuals, there is a tendency to neglect them (kind of like that economic analogy to the rental car, i.e., "nobody ever washed a rental car"). Have your cleaning company or a concierge service walk by these spaces regularly to ensure they are tidy and well stocked with cleaning and office supplies.
- *Provide a variety of space types to support the full range of work.* If the "alternative environments" you are creating look like Dil-

bertville, you've missed the point. Alternative environments reach their full potential when they are a rich mix of meeting spaces, team areas, cafés, phone booths, drop-in stations, soft seating areas, and the like.

- *Provide furniture components (like filing, lockers, and storage) to support the workplace solution.* If spaces are not assigned to individuals, they will require some storage to get work done. Once employees are mobile, they become very savvy at saving documents electronically, but there may still be some documents that need to be stored on site.
- *Conduct the appropriate research to support migration to an alternate work environment.* If you are an employee that wants to jump into alternative work methods right away, this is possible, but worth discussing more with your supervisor to make sure you have the tools and support you need.

Keys to success for off-premises solutions:

- *Provide ways for employees to sustain regular interaction with co-workers.* If you or members of your group are working off-site, even for a limited amount of time, it is important to maintain regular meetings (virtual or in-person) to keep in contact with each other. Communication is critical to a highly collaborative, effective knowledge workforce.
- *Create discipline in maintaining communications.* Most groups with remote employees choose to have regular weekly or bi-weekly meetings with each other in order to maintain a connection.
- *Investigate and mitigate insurance and liability issues.* Working at home can be a great solution for both employee and employer if it is appropriate for the employee's job function. However, it is important to obtain the right ergonomic furniture and equipment so that there is no physical discomfort while working at home. Also, some organizations dealing with sensitive material may require employees to have a separate room in the home where they can work or a lockable cabinet. Most employers generally require parents to put their younger

children in daycare or hire a nanny at home so that employees can be fully engaged in work.

- *Get middle management buy-in.* Senior leaders are often thrilled to adopt alternative work strategies because of the significant real-estate and operating cost savings. They may be frequent travelers themselves and see great benefits to offering this to individuals. Line managers or supervisors are generally not as open to off-site work options because they will lose physical access to their staff. Clear, objective performance metrics are critical to being able to manage teams remotely.

- *Establish new IT protocols (help desk, file management, ongoing training).* The most common complaint from individuals working from home or in some other facility besides their home office is regarding technology, i.e., that it's not working. And when there is a breakdown, employees will need a number to call or possibly have an IT technician come to them. In the office, employees may receive regular upgrades, training, or general education just by being there. Remote employees need just as much attention on this front.

- *Implement a robust communication and change management plan.* This goes for on- and off-site strategies. Some employees may already be working or wanting to work in this new way and will shout in unison, "it's about time" when they see their organization move to a more flexible work approach overall. Many others are creatures of habit and will see this new way of doing things as a threat to their position or to their productivity. This spectrum of reactions is absolutely natural and must be accommodated. Many organizations choose to pilot these strategies with eager groups before rolling them out more broadly.

Candidates for Alternative Work

Alternative work strategies are not for everyone. Organizations must weigh the functional ability of teams and individual workers to work remotely with cultural impact to the organization.

Here is a process for identifying the best candidates:

Figure 10.2

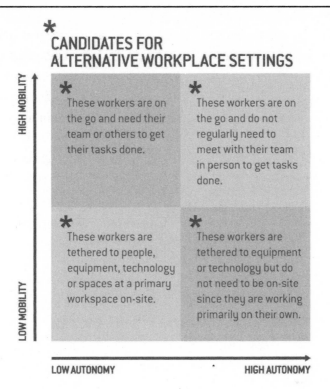

FUNCTIONAL ASSESSMENT

Assessing purely from a functional perspective, the two key attributes that must be considered are degree of mobility (how mobile these individuals are already) and level of autonomy (how much they depend on continuous feedback from their team to get work done). Figure 10.2 illustrates how this plays out at a high level. Candidates in the bottom left are likely to require a permanent seat in the office because they require face-to-face interaction with other employees and are tethered to equipment, technology, or their work setting in some way. Candidates in the other three quadrants could be candidates for an alternative work strategy, though not necessarily.

Cultural Assessment

Once a functional assessment has occurred, management should assess organizational readiness to adopt alternative workplace strategies in the context of existing culture. A large part of this readiness has to do with management style as much as it does with employees' ability to functionally work in a distributed way. Factors in Table 10.2 should be taken into consideration.

According to Kevin Kelly with the U.S. General Services Administration:

> People who are self-starters can be mobile and highly productive at the same time. They can interact when they need to interact—through scheduled meetings or via mobile technology. These individuals may be far more productive out of the office than they would be working through constant interruptions in an office setting. But alternative work is not for every kind of person or every kind of work style. Mobile work requires trust and protocols such as scheduled team meetings to ensure that it works. Perhaps most importantly, it requires supervisors to have a good sense of their employees' abilities and to set goals based on performance, not attendance. Allowing remote work may be one way to right-size the workspace, as well as to allow it to be energy-efficient, pleasant and as efficient as possible.[6]

The cultural change and communication required to roll out an alternative workplace program can take some time, but once your organization is thinking differently about how to support alternative work arrangements, consider opening up the dialogue to finding additional ways the company can collectively save resources and help benefit the environment.

The Implications of Alternative Work

Some companies have adopted alternative work approaches for the entire organization. Others have only adopted it for small groups. Regardless of the number of adopters in your organization, taking on strategies like these when appropriate can provide significant benefits to employees, the environment, and the bottom line. But what does embracing alternative work really mean for you?

Table 10.2   Evaluating Cultural Readiness to Adopt
             Alternative Work Strategies

Cultural Considerations	Questions to Ask
Goals and objectives of the team	Will the goals of the team be compromised by moving to an alternative work model?
Existing team dynamics	How disruptive will an alternative work model be to current team communication and camaraderie?
	What changes will need to be made to ensure that this dynamic will continue?
Time-management skills	Do employees have the discipline to manage their time remotely?
	Will they need to be trained in these skills prior to working from home either part-time or full-time?
Leadership style	Are leaders managing their staff remotely already or is this a totally new management challenge for them?
	Does leadership have the desire, willingness, or skill to manage a team remotely?
	Do they have the ability to manage and influence others without sitting next to them?
Ability to manage change	Does this team have the ability to work through the change management issues related to moving from traditional work to alternative work?
High-level written and verbal communication skills	Does this team have the written and verbal skills to communicate effectively virtually?
	Do team members have the ability to use the tools available to them to get their job done?
Ability and motivation to be an active and contributing part of a team	Will team members feel unconnected and unmotivated as part of a virtual team?
Technical knowledge	Does the individual or subgroup have the technical knowledge to work without constant interaction with their team?
	Do they need mentorship or can they take on tasks with little support from others?

IT'S ABOUT DOING MORE WITH LESS

Successful alternative work strategies reduce the amount of square feet required per employee. Ideally, workers are provided with healthy, beautiful spaces and effective tools and the right settings to get work done, but they might not be as large on a per-person basis as they are in a traditional environment. When moving from a traditional space to an alternative work environment, space metrics change from "square feet per person" to "square feet per person served." Space utilization for a traditionally assigned workforce can be around 230 square feet per person, whereas in a highly mobile environment it can easily be 100 square feet per person served. This means that a flexible space can accommodate two to three times the number of employees in the same amount of real estate. Nortel's Integrated Work Environment program has resulted in space that is 25 percent more efficient than their traditional portfolio—a savings that goes right to the bottom line. The recent relocation of the company's world headquarters in Toronto, Canada realized a 50 percent reduction in space per person served thanks to alternative work strategies.[7]

YOU MUST MANAGE TOWARD DIFFERENT GOALS

Some managers believe that they must see their employees every day in the office in order to manage them well. Often this is due to the unique functions of the organization that require face-to-face collaboration. It could also be because employees are new to the organization and either need mentorship or require additional training, introducing them to the organizational culture. There are also a large number of managers who resist letting their workforce work virtually because there are no clear performance metrics in place. Without clear standards of measurement, it is very difficult to manage remotely and trust members of your team to deliver. Managers that evaluate employees based on productivity, sales, or quality of deliverables rather than whether they are physically in the office are more likely to be open to virtual work alternatives.

Mobility at Cisco

Cisco's mobile work environment is referred to as the Cisco Connected Workplace (CCW) and it integrates the physical workplace and Internet Protocol Telephony plus other technologies. The CCW incorporates mobility strategies throughout the building from the desktop user through to the basement to ensure a connected strategy. In the workplace, each team is allocated a range of workplaces—workstations, dedicated team rooms, quiet space, and shared facilities.

Cisco has embraced mobility for its cost and environmental benefits. For example, managers in Europe have carbon targets on travel and energy use in their buildings and are evaluated on their ability to minimize real estate costs. Business units are charged "rent" by the corporate office for their workspace, so the smaller the footprint of the team the less they are charged back. Managers who save space see an impact to their bottom line and meet their environmental targets at the same time.

Cisco managers must adjust their mobility strategies based on the functions of their workforce as well as real estate drivers like rent costs. For example, Cisco has two major facilities in the London metropolitan area, one in the city of London (center city) and one in Bedfont Lakes (on the outskirts of London, near Heathrow). Cisco's offices in London are located in the NatWest Tower, one of the most expensive locations in the city. Cisco management could only justify leasing this prime piece of real estate if the space required was minimized. This was achieved by pushing the sharing ratios to three or four people per desk. This worked well, given that the employees working in the city were primarily sales staff and in and out of the office all day—the physical office space was just a place for them to touch down.

At Bedfont Lakes, employees tended to come to the site for one or two day periods, packing in their forecasting, team meetings, and training at the same time. This changed the way Cisco allocated space there versus the model used in its sales location. When Bedfont Lakes was first designed, the space standard was twenty square meters (sixty-five square feet) per person, but it is now only fourteen square meters (forty-five square feet) per person. Some Cisco offices in European countries house their employees in nine square meters (thirty square feet) per person. The Cisco Asia-Pacific offices also have a very low space per person standard. By working through alternative work strategies, the company has greatly impacted the utilization of its buildings worldwide.[8]

IT IS THE ULTIMATE GREEN WORKPLACE STRATEGY

This recent exploration and investment in alternative work goes hand in hand with green thinking. Companies that construct or rent space based on how their buildings are typically occupied as opposed to building for "peak occupancy" are leveraging all of the elements that go into a high performance green workspace including space, technology, policies and procedures, and operational strategies to improve their business and decrease their environmental footprint. They are also likely considering the green benefits of less travel to the office, which reduces both carbon emissions and costs for employees.

Transportation Demand Management

A large part of the workplace's impact on the environment comes not directly from the workplace itself, but from the act of getting to work. Americans spend an average of over one hundred hours per year commuting to and from their office.[9] Seventy-seven percent of those commuting hours are spent alone in a single occupant vehicle.[10] In addition, U.S. vehicle miles traveled for commuting to work increased from 4,180 miles per capita per year in 1969 to 5,720 miles per year in 2001, an increase of 37 percent.[11]

To reduce the environmental impact of commuting, many organizations have investigated Transportation Demand Management (TDM) strategies and policies to more efficiently use transportation resources or reduce demand for transportation in the first place. These TDM initiatives encourage individuals to reduce the number of trips they make, to use non-driving travel alternatives more often, to travel outside peak periods, and to reduce the distance and duration of their trips.

Transportation Demand Management is described explicitly in the Intermodal Surface Transportation Efficiency Act of 1994 (ISTEA), in the Clean Air Act Amendments of 1990, and in numerous local traffic reduction ordinances, development agreements, and transportation plans. While typically thought of as an urban planning measure, or something that is the purview of municipalities, TDM strategies can also be applied to the workplace no matter how large or small the office.

There are many different TDM strategies, which typically fall into three categories: incentives for using transportation other than single occupant vehicles (SOVs); disincentives for using SOVs; or overall reduction in number of trips. While all three have proven to be successful, the most successful TDM programs include a combination of strategies.

Providing incentives for alternate modes of transportation can be a powerful motivator for getting employees out of single occupant vehicles. Some of these alternative modes and related incentives include:

BICYCLING

Bicycling not only decreases the carbon footprint, but also helps riders in their personal goals: losing weight; exercising more; increasing energy; and setting a good example for kids. In order to encourage bicycling, employers can provide information, equipment facilities, and other incentives for people to bike to work. Examples of motivators include rebates for bicycle and accessory purchases, free tune-ups, discounts on bicycle clothes, and guidance on good resources that explain how to be a successful and safe bicyclist.

WALKING

Walking has many of the same benefits of bicycling, particularly in terms of better health through additional exercise. Companies are looking to locate in walkable communities not just to make the commute easier for employees: Having a location that is close to restaurants, shops, banks, dry cleaners, transit, and hotels not only saves the company on carbon emissions, but can increase productivity. Having those amenities close to the office will encourage employees to take a quick break—providing exercise, stimulation, and access to fresh air and natural light. Deborah Brown-Volkman, a career coach, claims, "it turns out giving up your lunch break could actually diminish your productivity, causing you to end up putting in more hours in the long run, not to mention what it does for your health and well being."[12] Web sites like Walk Score (www.walkscore.com) allow users to plug in an address to determine how "walkable" or accessible to amenities their office is.

MASS TRANSIT

Most metropolitan areas have buses and usually some sort of heavy or light rail system. Making these modes cheaper, more convenient, or otherwise more accessible is a great way to encourage ridership. Google provides shuttle bus service on biodiesel-fueled buses from San Francisco and its suburbs to its Mountain View headquarters. In addition to being green, these buses provide employees with a comfortable ride that includes free wireless Internet access, adding hours of potential productivity through a pleasant commute. On the public-sector side, the federal government offers employees $115 a month in transit vouchers, and also offers incentives to employers to do the same: Internal Revenue Service Revenue Procedure 2003–85 Qualified Transportation Fringe offers credits to employers who offer benefits for transportation in a commuter highway vehicle or through distribution of transit passes. Many state governments take this a step further and provide tax incentives to employers who offer transit benefits. The State of Maryland allows businesses to claim a 50 percent tax credit for the cost of providing commuter fringe benefits to its employees up to a maximum credit of $50 per participating employee per month. Through its Smart Moves for Business program, the State of New Jersey also offers a tax credit based on the amount of commuter transportation benefits awarded.

CARPOOL/VANPOOL/RIDESHARE

Another way to help reduce SOV commuting is to provide preferential treatment for those who engage in carpooling, such as premium parking spaces or low or no parking costs. Companies may also enable employees to make connections through carpool boards or Web sites. Some metropolitan areas already have existing carpool services, such as Commuter Connections in Washington, D.C. Washington, D.C. even has an unofficial carpool connection, known as "slug lines." Commuters line up at designated "slug areas" and people with cars needing extra bodies to qualify for HOV (high occupancy vehicle) lanes pick them up. The driver benefits by being permitted in HOV lanes, and the passengers benefit from the free car ride.

Hybrid vehicles

Many companies offer incentives for people to use hybrid (or biofuel or electric or other nongas) vehicles rather than the regular old gas guzzlers. This can be done through parking incentives: either reduced fees for parking, or preferred parking spots. Some companies have even gone so far as to provide cash incentives or rebates for the purchase of hybrid vehicles, including Google, Bank of America, and Timberland.[13]

Car share service

Another incentive for using nontraditional transportation is to provide car share services (such as Zipcar). HOK's Washington, D.C. office has a Zipcar account with free access to all employees, enabling those who typically do not drive to work the option of using one of these cars to travel to midday meetings or appointments, rather than bringing in their own car.

While incentives are a great way to get people to consider using alternate transportation modes, it is sometimes difficult to convince them that not driving is a viable option. Many municipalities and employers have turned to making commuting by single occupancy vehicle more difficult in order to encourage more sustainable transportation behaviors.

Most of the disincentives of TDM revolve around cost and convenience. The number one disincentive is parking: In order to convince commuters not to drive single occupancy vehicles, parking a car must be too difficult or expensive. The primary means of this include providing unattractive parking options for traditional vehicles, no parking at all, or by charging rates higher than the costs associated with alternate modes of transportation.

In 2003, London embraced the idea of travel disincentives with its "Congestion Charge." The main objectives of this charge were to reduce congestion, and to raise funds for investment in London's transport system. Vehicles entering a clearly defined zone of central London between the hours of 7:00 a.m. and 6:00 p.m., Monday to Friday, have to pay a fee of roughly £8 daily. Payment of the charge allows drivers to enter, drive within, and exit the Charging Zone that day. In addition, the city council in London's borough of Richmond has begun a policy where cars with more emissions pay bigger parking fees. Under the plan, the cars generating higher toxic emissions will be charged about a dollar an hour more to park than hybrids like the Toyota Prius. Richmond officials estimate the parking price-hike will affect 40 percent of cars.[14]

Corporate Travel

One thing TDM does not take into consideration explicitly is corporate travel. Many jobs require travel, but it is more essential to some job functions than others. Companies understand that travel is important to developing and maintaining relationships both within the company and with clients and partners. However, many are looking into options to reduce the carbon footprint associated with business travel.

Some of the ways communities and companies are reducing their travel carbon footprints include: travel policies that encourage the use of public transit or bundling of trips; discouraging unnecessary travel; encouraging virtual meetings and video conference technologies; requesting that employees select the mode of transportation that will have the least environmental impact; and purchasing offsets. The best policies around are comprehensive and incentivize green behavior.

Integrating TDM into the Business

Nortel and Texas Instruments are two organizations that have shown an exemplary commitment to transportation demand management at the corporate level.

GreenCommute at Nortel

Nortel has an advanced TDM program called GreenCommute. This program is used as a strategy at Nortel's worldwide locations, and involves engagement with local municipalities and transit authorities to improve service and integrate biking and walking trails. The program aims to change the modal split between drivers and people using other modes of transportation. The major benefits include a decrease in the number of cars on roads, as well as reduced requirements for asphalt on site.

To increase participation in GreenCommute, Nortel employs ongoing marketing and communication to its employees. The company hosts periodic competitions to "juice up the energy" around the program and encourage participation. Nortel has also participated in Canada's commuter challenge. This program has cities and corporations competing with each other to see who has the most evolved strategy and commuters..

Elements of the GreenCommute program include:

- Direct transit routing (minimizing bus and people travel distance)
- Web site "transit hub," complete with all the current route and schedule information, including a computerized link to the local transit agency with a screen showing pending arrival times, similar to an airport
- Cycling pathway network
- Dedicated carpool parking
- Shower, locker, and changing room facilities
- Signage for commuter or hybrid parking spaces
- Comprehensive Intranet site with transportation information
- On-line ride-matching system
- Drop-in areas for mobile workers

While there were many challenges in implementing this effort, including limited public transportation options in some locations, Nortel has found great success with the GreenCommute program:

- Strong employee support of GreenCommute and increased acceptance of sustainable commuting modes
- High level of participation in the national Commuter Challenge
- Numerous awards for Nortel: 2004 US EPA Best Workplaces for Commuters standard of excellence designation (Research Triangle Park and Billerica); 1999–2006 Top Private Sector Employer in Ottawa National Commuter Challenge; Alfred P. Sloan Work/Life Award (RTP); 2006 TravelWise Leadership Award (Ottawa); and 2006 National Clean Air Day Award (Canada)
- Increase of non-driving commuters in the first two years from 20 percent to 25 percent

Texas Instruments' (TI) Employee Trip Reduction program

In 1996, TI's Dallas-based Employee Trip Reduction program was set in motion. Texas Instruments provides educational training, on-site facilities, and services that encourage employees to make fewer small trips in their cars during the day. This includes a range of strategies, such as flexible work schedules, shuttle service, and advanced communications technology to help reduce employee trips between work sites. Available to about one-third of the company's employees, most of whom reside in the North Texas area, this program has continued to grow steadily. In 2007, for an investment of $1.5 million, TI's trip-reduction efforts kept an estimated 8,400 vehicles off North Texas roads daily, a Texas-sized step in the right direction.

Commuting coordinators at high-population facilities such as those in Manchester, New Hampshire and Tucson, Arizona assist with employee trip reduction and awareness activities. Texas Instruments provides bus service for employees in the Philippines. In France, TI hosts a Web site to educate workers on commuting options. The site includes an eco-calculator to help employees calculate the annual costs of their transportation options.[15]

Enrolling managers and staff to adopt alternative work approaches takes some effort and requires a real understanding of their work needs. Addressing alternative transportation options is no different. Employees have kids to drop off at school and get to soccer practice. They have commitments with clients, business trips to work in, and complex logistics to be sorted out just to enable them to get to work. In the same way that not everyone is a candidate for alternative work, not every day will be appropriate for leaving the car at home. But even biking, walking, busing, or carpooling just one day a week can really help make a difference in air quality in cities. Similarly, reducing the number of longer range business trips by three or four a year will help reduce environmental impact at a global level, and will give employees more time with their families.

So now that you have transformed your workplace into a totally new kind of environment, what's next? What happens if everyone starts thinking this way? What will this mean for the way people communicate, the way they conduct business, and how society behaves in general?

Actions You Can Take Today

1. Identify your company's current policies for alternative work and see if any of them make sense for your job. Approach your supervisor about possible opportunities to save you and the team time and money.
2. Investigate whether your organization has special parking privileges for alternative fuel vehicles or carpools. Sign up if you qualify.
3. Take the train or bus next week (whichever might be available to you). If none of these are a viable option, carpool.
4. Map out a bike route or walk to work next week if it is viable option. Try some of these sites for more information:

   - Bikely (maps for biking to work safely): www.bikely.com
   - The Green Commute (make a pledge to bike more): http://green-bikes.net/index.html

CHAPTER 11

The Green Workplace
of the Future

We should all be concerned about the future because we will have to spend
the rest of our lives there.

—Charles F. Kettering, American inventor and
the holder of over 300 patents

Much of this book has focused on strategies that are designed to create
more sustainable workplaces, but within today's constraints. Thus, although many of these strategies are cutting edge and transformative, they
are still built within the context of existing infrastructure, policies, and cultural norms. To become better stewards of our environment, and to build
sustainability plans that are themselves "sustainable" over the long term, it's
critical that we also plan for a future set of parameters. What will workplaces look like ten, fifty, or a hundred years from now? How will our environment be able to sustain them? And how will employees, managers,
and executives need to change how they work, live, and play to be effective
in this future?

To put this in context, think about major innovations that have happened over the last few centuries and how quickly they have changed how we work. Consider some of the highlights:

1023   First paper money printed in China.

1202   Hindu–Arabic numbering system introduced to the West by Italian mathematician, Fibonacci.

1436   Johannes Gutenberg invents printing press with metal movable type.

1543   Copernicus publishes his theory that the earth is not the center of the universe.

1792   William Murdoch invents gas lighting.

1800   Count Alessandro Volta invents the battery.

1807   Humphry Davy invents the first electric light, called an arc lamp.

1814   George Stephenson designs the first steam locomotive.

1829   American W. A. Burt invents the typewriter.

1841   Samuel Slocum patents the stapler.

1843   Alexander Bain of Scotland invents the facsimile.

1861   Ernest Michaux invents the bicycle.

1876   Alexander Graham Bell patents the telephone.

1901   The first radio receiver successfully receives a radio transmission.

1902   Willis Carrier invents the air conditioner.

1908   Model T first sold.

1938   Chester F. Carlson invents the photocopier.
        First jet engine is built.

1959   Jack Kilby and Robert Noyce both invent the microchip.

1965   Compact disc invented by James Russell.

1972   Word processor invented.

1973   Ethernet (local computer network) invented by Robert Metcalfe and Xerox.

1979   Cell phone invented.

1981   First IBM PC invented.

1984	Apple Macintosh invented.
1991	World Wide Web invented by Tim Berners-Lee and Robert Cailliau.
1991	U.S. government offers Internet access to the general public for the first time.
	First commercial short message service (SMS) message is sent in the UK.
1995	DVD (Digital Versatile Disc or Digital Video Disc) invented.
1998	Google started by Larry Page and Sergey Brin in Menlo Park, California.
1999	BlackBerry invented by a professor at Waterloo University in Ontario.
2001	Apple Computers publicly announces its portable music digital player—the iPod.
2001	Toyota's Prius hit the U.S. market.
2004	Harvard University student Mark Zuckerberg invents Facebook.

Think about all of these completely transformative innovations and how our lives at work and home have been forever changed because of them. Just over a hundred years ago, people didn't expect buildings to have air conditioning. Just thirty years ago, there were no cell phones to get connected, and just twenty years ago there was no Web to surf the latest news. The acceleration of the impact of these innovations is also profound. It took radio thirty-eight years to gain an audience of 50 million; it took Facebook two. The first commercial text message was sent in 1992; the total sent each day now exceeds the total population of the planet.[1]

Predictions

It's hard to believe how quickly the world has become accustomed to a technology-rich and lighting-fast paced way of life. Each of these innovations gave us a solution to a problem of the day—faster travel, more comfort, and quicker access to knowledge. Now that we are facing major environmental problems, can we leverage—even accelerate—this same innovative spirit in search of solutions?

THE NEXT ECONOMIC SHIFT WILL BE TO A SOCIETY OF IDEAS

There have been dramatic shifts over the last several hundred years that have profoundly altered the ways that economic and social activities take place. Those shifts have not always been consistent across disparate societies, but, in general, they have led countries and regions from economies that are agriculturally based (centered on farming) to economies that are industrially based (centered on factory production) to economies focused on information (centered on knowledge work). The type of economy you live in determines the kind of work you do, how you support your family, the business relationships you maintain, and the education you need. Many believe the next shift (post-knowledge work) will be built around an economy of creativity and new ideas. Armed with technology, global access, and the need to differentiate in a highly competitive marketplace, people with creative minds and the ability to synthesize and collaborate with others effectively will be the ones who succeed.

What is driving the movement to this new economy? Alan Greenspan, former chairman of the Federal Reserve Board, recognized the role of "conceptual output" in 1997 in a speech at the University of Connecticut when he said, "The growth of the conceptual component of output has brought with it accelerating demands for workers who are equipped not simply with technical know-how, but with the ability to create, analyze, and transform information and to interact effectively with others."[2] By 2004, he expanded on these remarks, referring to reductions in manufacturing in the United States, outsourcing to India and China, and an excess of supply and the global marketplace all leading to the increasing conceptualization of economic output.[3] Since then, a number of influential writers and thinkers have predicted the movement away from the knowledge economy to one of concepts and ideas, including Thomas Friedman in *The World Is Flat* and Daniel Pink in *The Whole New Mind.*

So if a conceptual or idea-based economy is inevitable, and creativity, innovation, and design are the methods for creating value in this economy, what does this mean in terms of transforming the workplace? For starters, it may mean that the best physical and virtual offices will be ones that support extreme face-to-face collaboration. The most effective physical setting for work may need to resemble a theater as opposed to the more rigid workplace environments built today. The theater—a flexible and dynamic space with unique props to support collaboration—could be the perfect setting for stimulating and spawning new ideas. Virtual environments, the complement to physical spaces, may require enhanced social networking and visualization tools to become more engaging and interactive than they are today.

The advent of the idea-based economy may impact more than just the setting for work; it may also change how work happens altogether. For example, using inductive or deductive thinking (proving things that already exist) to solve the same old problems may not get the results needed to thrive in a setting that will increasingly demand new ideas altogether. Further, when it comes to our environmental challenges in particular, the issues may simply be too large, too complex, and too integrated to solve through linear thinking and pure logic alone. Design thinking, on the other hand, is a perfect tool for "shooting a moving target," i.e., solving problems and achieving creative outcomes in a rapidly changing set of conditions. The very attributes of design thinking—synthesis, visualizing possibilities, making hypotheses, looking for complex issues to solve, balancing requirements versus possibilities, and being open to scrutiny—are all particularly timely and relevant for creating value in a concept-based economy.

According to Bill Valentine, Chairman of HOK: "In the future, we will be an idea-based culture and all menial tasks we now perform in offices will be taken care of virtually. We'll have really smart people leading the world and social structures stemming from ideas—people will be able to work any place they want. It's the *ideas* that are the most important thing in keeping the world together as it grows and changes and there are more urgent problems to solve." [4]

THERE WILL ALWAYS BE A NEED FOR FACE-TO-FACE INTERACTION

Even with the trend toward increased virtualization, face-to-face interaction is not going away. Having direct, eye-to-eye communication with people is particularly important, especially when business depends on strong global relationships across cultures and regions. For really important meetings, people will need to exchange ideas with their physical presence, something that goes beyond words. Thus, some degree of face-to-face will always be essential for establishing trust and building sustainable relationships.

Judith Heerwagen, environmental and evolutionary psychologist, claims:

> One thing that will remain constant about the future of work—it will continue to be about relationships. The real value will be the social relationships that occur when people are together in one place. It is difficult to develop these virtually. Meeting colleagues in person lets you know how they will react in situations or with other people and is particularly important for making sound business judgments. Virtual communication is not always a viable substitute.[5]

This need to be face-to-face implies that there will continue to be a need for a physical setting for people to interact, although where it is, how it looks, and when it is used may change. Chris Hood, Hewlett-Packard's Workplace Program Manager, suggests: "We should be thinking about the facilitation of people, connectivity and spaces for groups. Organizations in the future should explore the value of putting people together. Offices should be more flexible, like a kit of parts. Footprints will be smaller and more focused on the interaction between people. Materials will be much friendlier to the environment—more deconstructable and reusable."[6]

At HP, where being green and challenging the status quo is encouraged from the Chief Executive Office (CEO) on down as simply being good business, 30 to 40 percent of the company's 321,000 people wake up and ask, "Where will I work today?" The answer is determined by business, cultural, and personal drivers, says Hood. "HP does not tell employees where to work—it only matters that they are productive." Aggressively reducing its physical space needs through sharing, free address, and reconfigured labs has sparked a happy collision of environmental and cost-saving benefits. HP employees continue to come to work with some regularity to get that face-to-face time, but where they go and when they meet has become much more flexible and fluid, and based on need, not entitlement.[7]

WORK WILL HAPPEN EVERYWHERE

Today, despite the wide availability of mobile work, many still believe that "If I am not sitting at my desk, I am not working." That may have been true decades ago, but it is not true today. Many workers still put a significant emphasis on their individual office as the only setting for getting work done. For a self-motivated knowledge worker, having a single place to work is not necessarily the most stimulating or productive arrangement. According to Kevin Kelly with the U.S. General Services Administration, offices may be very different in the future.

> Many workplace experts believe that the future will be part nineteenth-century social club—a comfortable place where workers can go for exchange of information and even camaraderie; part Kinko's, where equipment is readily available to effectively serve workers on the go; and part library carrel for concentrative work. It will be more open and more flexible, aided by white noise technology that greatly improves the speech privacy of open arrangements at low cost. The office of the future will not follow a one-size-fits-all, factory-like approach that characterizes the misuse of the work station that has flourished since the 1970's. Even Robert Probst, the prime inventor of the modern workstation, claimed that the open office has become "monolithic insanity" before he died in 2001. Alternative work environments, such as a home office, a coffee shop, a library, a convention center, an airport or a chair in the back yard with a Black-Berry nearby may be the right mix of settings to support real creativity and happiness on the job while greatly benefiting the environment.[8]

With clever use of infrastructure, natural resources, good change management, and training, it may be possible in the future to use significantly less overall real estate to conduct business, while still providing more options for getting work done and supporting workers' unique lifestyle and work function. And when they do need to get together to be effective, according to Dave Dunn in Workplace Planning, Innovation and Construction at Nortel, workers will be purposely coming to a place to "congregate, collaborate and create together, to socialize and to be entertained. Heads-down work just happens wherever they feel the most self-actualized, relaxed, and positive. The degree to which technology will allow that collaboration to take place virtually will have a big impact."[9]

THERE WILL BE AN EMPHASIS ON LOCAL INVESTMENT

Being good stewards of the environment means thinking locally. This means using nearby energy and water resources, buying local products and services, and providing local jobs. Knowledge work has created the need for highly specialized subject matter experts with unique skills, which, in turn, has increased the amount of time workers are on the road, sharing their knowledge over a global platform. Many organizations believe that exclusivity is valuable and to find the best consultant or best talent they must "fly the specialists in" rather than build this expertise within their own team or region. A surprising number of specialists can be found locally, especially if the organization makes an investment to train local workers. Often, investing in local knowledge and talent is much more sustainable (and affordable in the long run) than investing in dispersed talent. Further, beyond "going local," companies will increasingly have a wide range of options for supporting environmentally friendly (a.k.a. green-collar) jobs overall. What kinds of green-collar jobs can your organization support? Here are a few:

- Green architects and builders
- Recycling and reclamation companies
- Renewable energy companies
- Regional public transportation agencies
- Organic farmers and growers
- Green office suppliers
- Green cleaning companies

GREEN THINKING WILL BE MAINSTREAM

Most experts agree that the environmental issues we face today are not going away anytime soon, so third-party accreditation requirements like Leadership in Energy and Environmental Design (LEED), Building Research Establishment Environmental Assessment Method (BREEAM), Energy Star, and Green Globes are quickly becoming normal business practice. Wide, sweeping mandates to reduce carbon footprint and energy use are only becoming more stringent. This will mean that businesses will need to get creative and work hard to stay within these narrowing constraints. For example, sourcing energy and water more locally will be increasingly important to enable organizations to meet federal, state, or local targets. Randy Knox, at Adobe Systems Inc., is anticipating the need for corporations to step up and adopt new methods for creating renewable energy in particular. "Energy must be generated on site to maximize efficiency. So companies like Adobe need to start planning for that. We are looking at installing a fuel cell in one of our tower buildings. We might even start to see buildings designed around an onsite energy source."[10]

Although some skeptics say the "environmental movement" is just a fad, most organizations are betting the environmental issues we face today will be here for the long term. How do we know this?

- The United Nations reports that global investment in renewable energy was a record $148.4 billion in 2007, jumping 60 percent from 2006. Most clean-energy investing is happening in Europe, followed by the United States, China, India, and Brazil, and is still going full-throttle despite turmoil in the global financial markets. Investment is expected to reach $450 billion a year by 2012, rising to more than $600 billion a year by 2020.[11]
- In the United States, the Obama administration is making energy policy, environmental targets, and the creation of green-collar jobs a top priority. Most political pundits agree these measures will need to be dramatic in order to provide economic stimulus and lessen America's dependence on foreign energy sources.
- Lifestyles of Health and Sustainability (LOHAS) is the marketplace for goods and services focused on health, the environment, social justice, personal development, and sustainable living. The Natural Marketing Institute states that the over $200 billion industry is on track to grow to $420 billion in just three years and could accelerate to $845 billion by 2015.[12]
- Since the U.S. Green Building Council launched its LEED certification program in 2000, the number of certified and registered projects has grown dramatically. At the end of 2007, the square footage

of U.S. office and commercial space registered or certified under LEED totaled 2.3 billion, up more than 500 percent from two years earlier.[13]

- Although specific future government regulation and mandates are difficult to predict, in general, more aggressive environmental legislation vis-à-vis reduced energy use and carbon emissions is widely expected. The Dingell-Boucher draft bill, for example, proposed a gradual tightening of U.S. emissions standards to produce an 80 percent reduction in greenhouse gas emissions (as measured in 2005) by 2050.[14] While the specifics of the bill and even the ultimate sponsors may change, it is clear that the bar is already being set far higher than in the past. Further, similar legislation is being considered or has already passed at the state and city level in many locations.

What do these trends mean for the workplace? Most likely, they will dramatically impact building requirements, transportation standards and incentives for increased use of renewable energy. More and more, there will be an expectation or even demand from employees, labor unions, and local governments that all workplaces must be significantly greener. Some compare the emergence of environmental concerns to previous concerns about accessibility for the disabled or workplace safety. At the time issues like asbestos, for example, were first uncovered, there was a great deal of attention, consternation, and even outright fear over what the financial implications might be. However, after a while, addressing them simply became part of business as usual.

In addition to pushing the envelope on more stringent energy and emissions targets, the marketplace will increasingly require workplaces to have healthy indoor environments with some degree of increased natural light, thermal comfort, and individual controls that allow workers to be at their productive best. Workers will simply come to expect this as a given, as opposed to a luxury. This is especially true of new buildings (more subject to legislation), but will increasingly be a requirement for existing building stock. Pressure to provide healthy work environments with a minimal impact on the environment is here to stay.

Moving Forward

With these major shifts ahead of us, how do employees, employers, and all of the industries that are benefiting from today's models change the way they do business? According to Jeff Austin, Senior Vice President of Sustainability Strategy at Wachovia Corporate Real Estate: "It can be difficult to go from 'reality to possibility' in the same moment. The major problem with green thinking in general is our dearth of imagination. We can't imagine the impacts of climate change. We can't imagine a different reality than today. Because we can't envision it, we won't work to fix it. Even in ancient writings, people failed due to lack of vision. It's so hard for individuals to see an end-to-end systemic view of the world."[15]

If people are limited by imagination, then it is probably time for employers and employees to spend more time honing their creative and abductive thinking skills. It's also time to bring in smart people from outside of your core business practice to look at your business from a different perspective and to consider ways to transform the organization through education, training, and leadership.

Austin predicts: "Environmental issues will not be resolved through technological solutions, but rather by political decisions. Our leaders must engage in a larger conversation about issues in order to move us forward. Also, the bias of Western culture and a focus on the individual rather than the communal inhibits truly sustainable thinking."[16]

Even organizations well on their way to transforming the way they work will face many challenges ahead. Over the past several years, HP has gone through a significant workplace transformation. As far as the company has come, however, there are still many green workplace projects and initiatives that are only in planning stages. Chris Hood claims: "We cannot just snap our fingers and have our workplace change overnight. In order to affect systematic change, we are launching a few projects that are truly leadership projects, and then we must convince everyone all over again. Local solutions are critical as part of this."[17]

REMEMBER TONY JONES from the first chapter? "Successful" by all traditional measures, and yet trapped in a stressful, very non-green life of long hours, long commutes, and personal sacrifice? Let's flash forward—way forward, to a point at which Tony has long since retired. His kids are now in their forties, living in a way Tony could have only dreamt of, and working in jobs that were only a twinkle in an economist's eye back in "Dad's day." Probably the best example is Tony's daughter, Susan, a successful analyst at a major renewable energy company.

Susan White grew up in suburbia—remember Tony's hard-earned six-bedroom house? She went to a top-notch private school and had everything a child could want—except time with her parents. As she entered her child-rearing years, she realized that she wanted to be around more for her kids. Thankfully, times have changed a great deal since her dad's tenure at Alpha, Inc. Susan works for Zeta Energy, a renewable energy conglomerate. Although the company is global, energy resources for the firm are local and managed locally, so most of her working relationships are within the city. Because of its mission and the company's focus on the bottom line, Susan rarely travels and is able to work at home most days, commuting to her "office" only for special meetings. At home, she works in a small area equipped with the latest technology—all the way down to a holograph replication of her physical office. Virtual office technology lets her know when her colleagues are available for a casual conversation or want to be left alone. It is never lonely working at home—she knows what everyone is up to and visual and written communication is constant. The hard part is turning off virtual communication for thoughtful reflection. Susan has her home surrounded with plants and natural light to keep her mind fresh. Luckily, she has a passion for nature and farming. So even though Susan lives on the top floor of a downtown high-rise, she harvests a beautiful vegetable garden on her patio (her building is a cooperative that supports vertical farming). Living in a green building not only makes her feel as if she is working in the middle of a park, but it provides affordable, healthy food for her and her family. Her daily routine revolves around her husband, her children, and the meetings she schedules to get projects done on time. Her parents say she's "lucky" because she isn't on the road all the time and works a regular thirty-hour week. Susan just thinks it's common sense to have a lifestyle that supports her personal choices. She really appreciates the hard work and sacrifices her parents made, but she is happy the world has embraced a different way of thinking.

WHERE WILL YOU be in thirty years? And what kind of work environment do you want your children to enjoy? Thinking ahead, what do you need to change today to create a more environmentally friendly, efficient, and productive workplace? How will infrastructure need to evolve? What "essential" components of work today will seem irrelevant if not downright silly in the green workplace of tomorrow? Are the buildings we see today with monochromatic cubicles and dim lighting the most inspiring and collaborative spaces available? What about working at a café, around a dining room table, in a theater or an art studio? The "typical" workplace of today may already have ceased to be the optimal setting for productivity. Perhaps it never really was. Ask yourself—when you need to get focused, really focused, what is the most effective environment for you? Is it a ten foot by twelve foot whitewalled cell (otherwise known as an office) or is it a library, a bookstore, or your living room sofa?

Even if you are not ready to permanently relocate yourself or your team to a coffee shop, consider the importance of technology, flexibility, and personal choice in increasing your productivity and happiness. The goal of the green workplace of the future should be to facilitate creative ideas, accommodate intense think time, and allow for a rich and rewarding work and personal life. It's about being less tethered, more meaningful, less stressed, more engaged, and more stimulating than the environments most people work in today.

But these changes cannot stop with you and your organization. Green workplaces must also use resources wisely—staying lean and appropriately sized to support a greater environmental responsibility. A green workplace in its truest sense enables a happier, healthier, and more environmentally aware workforce and community with the smallest ecological footprint possible. So what about your work and home life will need to change to make room for this? And, if you change, can you convince your colleagues, clients, stakeholders and family members to take on the challenge as well? The changes you make today and the changes made by people you influence will have a "ripple effect," yielding significant results in years to come. Start by learning more about environmental issues, taking specific actions, teaching others what you have learned, and working toward a greener tomorrow.

Take a new step each day, and eventually you may find that you've not only succeeded in greening your own workplace, but also that much larger workplace on which six billion people live, breathe, and work every day—Planet Earth.

Notes

Chapter 1: The Case for Change

1.   Bureau of Labor Statistics, *Employment Projections: 2006–16 Summary,* USDL 07–1847, Washington, D.C.: GPO, December 4, 2007: 3.

2.   Marco R. della Cava, "Working out of a 'Third Place'," *USA Today.com,* October 4, 2006, http://www.usatoday.com/tech/2006-10-04-third-space_x.htm/.

3.   Alicia (Real Estate Sustainability Manager, Sprint Nextel), in interview with the author, February 5, 2008.

4.   This 2007 estimate is from a historical government building in downtown Washington, D.C.

5.   Ross Moore, "Colliers International's 2008 Parking Rate Survey," Colliers International's 2008 Parking Rate Survey, July 14, 2008, http://www.colliers.com/Markets/Charlotte/News/2008_ParkingSurvey.

6.   Alex Wilson and Rachel Navaro, "Driving to Green Buildings: The Transportation Energy Intensity of Buildings," *Environmental Building News,* September 1, 2007, http://www.buildinggreen.com/auth/article.cfm/2007/8/30/Driving-to-Green-Buildings-T.

7.   "Doing Good: Business and the Sustainability Challenge," *The Economist Intelligence Unit 2008,* February 2008, p. 6, http://a330.g.akamai.net/7/330/25828/20080208191823/graphics.eiu.com/upload/Sustainability_allsponsors.pdf.

8.   Corporate sustainability is a business approach that creates long-term shareholder value by embracing opportunities and managing risks deriving from economic, environmental and social developments.

9.   Alicia Martin interview.

10. Gareth Vorster, "Corporate Social Responsibility Is More Important than Salary when Choosing a Job," *Personnel Today,* August 2, 2007, http://www.personneltoday.com/articles/2007/08/02/41767/corporate-social-responsibility-is-more-important-than-salary-when-choosing-a-job.html.

11. Justina Victor, "SHRM Survey Brief: Green Workplace," *Society for Human Resource Management,* January 2008, 3.

12. Matthew Kiernan and Paul Dickinson, "Carbon Disclosure Project Report 2007 Global FT500," Innovest Strategic Value Advisors and Carbon Disclosure Project (CDP) 2007, iii.

13.   "The 2006 Cone Millennial Cause Study The Millennial Generation: Pro-Social and Empowered to Change the World," By Cone Inc. in collaboration with AMP Insights, http://www.solsustainability.org/documents/toolkit/2006%20Cone%20Millennial%20Cause%20Study.pdf.

14.   "Gen Y's 15 Favorite Green Brands: From Food to Cars . . . from Clothes to Cleaning Supplies," *The Daily Green,* August 4, 2008, http://www.thedailygreen.com/environmental-news/latest/green-brands-47080404.

15.   Marc Gunther, "The Green Machine," *Fortune,* July 31, 2006, http://money.cnn.com/magazines/fortune/fortune_archive/2006/08/07/8382593/.

16.   Lisa Fay Matthiessen and Peter Morris, *Cost of Green Revisited: Reexamining the Feasibility and Cost Impact of Sustainable Design in the Light of Increased Market Adoption,* Davis Langdon, July 2007, p. 3, http://www.davislangdon.com/upload/images/publications/USA/The%20Cost%20of%20Green%20Revisited.pdf.

17.   James Feldman, "How Will Green Construction Affect REITs?," UBS Research, October 8, 2007, 3, 6.

18.   Feldman, "How Will Green Construction Affect REITs?"

19.   Paul Westbrook (Sustainable Development Manager for Texas Instruments International Facilities), in interview with the author, August 26, 2008.

20.   W. J. Fisk and A. H. Rosenfeld, "Estimates of Improved Productivity and Health from Better Indoor Environments," *Center for Building Science News* #18, Summer 1997, http://eetdnews.lbl.gov/cbs_nl/nl15/productivity.html.

21.   Jonathan Lash and Fred Wellington, "Competitive Advantage on a Warming Planet," *Harvard Business Review,* March 2007, 3–6.

22.   Don Horn (Sustainable Design Director, General Services Administration), in interview with the author, February 21, 2008.

23.   "Wal-Mart Takes Sustainability Efforts to Suppliers," *Environmental Leader,* February 2007, http://www.environmentalleader.com/2007/02/02/wal-mart-takes-sustainability-efforts-to-suppliers/.

24.   The Opus Group, "Why Green Building Has Staying Power," *2007 Green Building Survey, National Real Estate Investor and Retail Traffic,* November, 2007, 3, http://nreionline.com/brokernews/greenbuildingnews/green_building_survey/.

25.   U.S. Senate, *Federal and Private Insurers in Coming Decades Are Potentially Significant, Report to the Committee on Homeland Security and Governmental Affairs,* Government Accountability Office, Washington, D.C., GPO, March 2007: 17.

26.   "Investors: A New World of Risk and Opportunity," *Climate Action,* November 26, 2007, http://www.climateactionprogramme.org/features/article/investors_a_new_world_of_risk_and_opportunity/.

27.   Evan Mills, "From Risk to Opportunity: 2007 Insurer Responses to Climate Change," *A Ceres Report,* November 2007, 14–16.

28.   Melissa Orien and David Zimmerman, "Hot Trends and Even Hotter Litigation," *Construction Executive,* June 2008, 50.

29.   Thomas F. Segella, "'Sick Building' and 'Indoor Air Quality,'" *Federation of Insurance and Corporate Council Quarterly,* Spring 1999.

Chapter 2: The Global Picture

1.   E. O. Wilson, *The Future of Life* (New York: Vintage Books, 2002), 27.

2.   A global hectare (gha) is a measurement that is used to quantify biological productivity on a global scale. It is a unit used primarily to report the biocapacity of the earth

and to make conclusions about local biological demand that is independent of local biological productivity factors (thus normalized to a global scale). It is becoming more frequently used in geographic, environmental, and sociological circles, as it relates both to ecological footprint, and global development.

3. Data taken from the Global Footprint Network, http://www.footprintnetwork.org/.

4. Ann-Louise Martin and Paul Lashmar, "The Real Price of Water," UNESCO Sources, Number 101, May 1998, 5.

5. Rachel Oliver, "Measuring Your Water Footprint," *CNN.com*, October 6, 2008, http://edition.cnn.com/2008/TECH/10/03/eco.water.hoekstra/index.html/.

6. World Resources Institute, "Energy and Resources," *Earth Trends Energy and Resources Country Profiles Database, 2003,* http://earthtrends.wri.org/searchable_db/index.php?theme=6&variable_ID=351&action=select_countries.

7. Energy Information Administration, *Annual Energy Review 2005,* Washington, D.C.: GPO, July 2006: 27.

8. G.R. Matos, 2007, *Effects of Regulation and Technology on End Uses of Nonfuel Mineral Commodities in the United States: U.S. Geological Survey Scientific Investigations Report 2006–5194,* Reston, VA: U.S. Geological Survey, 2007 : 3.

9. Frederick W. Allen, "Material Flows in the United States: A Physical Accounting of the U.S. Industrial Ecology," Journal of Industrial Ecology, Volume 12 Issue 5–6, 2008a: 785–791.

10. L. A. Wagner, "Materials in the Economy—Material Flows, Scarcity and the Environment," U.S. Geological Survey Circular 1221, Denver, CO: U.S. Geological Survey, 2002: 7.

11. David Malin Lenssen and Nicholas Roodman, "Worldwatch Paper 124: A Building Revolution: How Ecology and Health Concerns Are Transforming Construction," Worldwatch Institute, March 1, 1995, http://www.worldwatch.org/node/866/.

12. Ahmed ElAmin, "Nestlé Cuts Water Use at Manufacturing Plants," *Foodproductiondaily.com,* March 19, 2007, http://www.foodproductiondaily.com/Processing/Nestle-cuts-water-use-at-manufacturing-plants/.

13. Energy Information Administration (EIA), Weekly United States Spot Price FOB Weighted by Estimated Import Volume (Dollars per Barrel), http://tonto.eia.doe.gov/dnav/pet/hist/wtotusaw.htm.

14. John Wood and Gary Long, *Long Term World Oil Supply (A Resource Base/Production Path Analysis),* report prepared for the Energy Information Administration, U.S. Department of Energy, July 28, 2007, http://tonto.eia.doe.gov/FTPROOT/presentations/long_term_supply/sld001.htm/.

15. Energy Information Administration, U.S. Department of Energy, *Renewable Energy Consumption and Electricity Preliminary 2007 Statistics,* Washington, D.C.: GPO, 2008.

16. Renewable Energy Policy Network for the 21st Century, "Renewables 2007: Global Status Report" (White Paper, 2007), http://www.ren21.net/pdf/RE2007_Global_Status_Report.pdf.

17. Ton-miles refer to a unit of freight transportation equivalent to a ton of freight moved one mile.

18. David L. Greene, Andreas Schafer, "Reducing Greenhouse Gas Emissions from U.S. Transportation," Pew Center on Global Climate Change, May 2003, http://www.pewclimate.org/docUploads/ustransp.pdf.

19. A light truck or light duty truck is a classification for trucks or truck-based vehicles with a payload capacity of less than 4,000 pounds.

20. Federal Highway Administration, U.S. Department of Transportation, *Highway Statistics 2001,* Washington, D.C.: GPO, 2001.

21. Organisation for Economic Co-operation and Development (OECD), "Environment Statistics: Municipal Waste Generation (Most Recent) by Country," Nation Master.com, http://www.nationmaster.com/graph/env_mun_was_gen-environment-municipal-waste-generation/.

22. U.S. Environmental Protection Agency, *Municipal Solid Waste Generation, Recycling, and Disposal in the United States: Facts and Figures for 2006,* Washington, DC: GPO, 2006.

23. Franklin Associate, *Characterization of Building-Related Construction and Demolition Debris in the United States,* report prepared for the U.S. EPA Municipal and Industrial Solid Waste Division Office of Solid Waste, June 1998.

24. U.S. Environmental Protection Agency, *Solid Waste Management and Greenhouse Gases: A Life-Cycle Assessment of Emissions and Sinks,* May 2002, http://epa.gov/climatechange/wycd/waste/downloads/fullreport.pdf.

25. U.S. Environmental Protection Agency, *Healthy Buildings, Healthy People: A Vision for the 21st Century,* October 2001, www.epa.gov/iaq/hbhp/hbhptoc.html/.

26. U.S. Environmental Protection Agency, *EPA Assessment of Risks from Radon in Homes,* June 2003, http://www.epa.gov/radon/risk_assessment.html /.

27. U.S. Environmental Protection Agency, *Respiratory Health Effects of Passive Smoking: Lung Cancer and Other Disorders,* 1993, oaspub.epa.gov/eims/eimscomm.getfile?p_download_id=36793.

28. Committee on the Assessment of Asthma and Indoor Air, Division of Health Promotion and Disease Prevention, Institute of Medicine, "Clearing the Air: Asthma and Indoor Air Exposures," Institute of Medicine, National Academy of Sciences, 2000, http://www.iom.edu/report.asp?id=5511

29. National Center for Health Statistics, Center for Disease Control, *2001 National Health Interview Survey (NHIS),* 2001, http://www.cdc.gov/nchs/products/pubs/pubd/hestats/asthma/asthma.htm/.

30. A high efficiency particulate air or HEPA filter can remove at least 99.97% of airborne particles.

31. Sick building syndrome is a combination of ailments associated with an individual's place of work (office building) or residence. Sick building causes are frequently pinned down to flaws in the heating, ventilation, and air conditioning (HVAC) systems. Other causes have been attributed to contaminants produced by outgassing of some types of building materials, volatile organic compounds, molds (see mold health issues), improper exhaust ventilation of light industrial chemicals used within, or fresh-air intake location / lack of adequate air filtration.

32. G. Kats, L. Alevantis, A. Berman, E. Mills, and J. Perlman, "The Costs and Financial Benefits of Green Buildings: A Report to California's Sustainable Building Taskforce," October 2003, http://www.cap-e.com/ewebeditpro/items/O59F3259.pdf.

33. Energy Information Administration, *Assumptions to the Annual Energy Outlook 2008: With Projections to 2030,* Washington, D.C.: GPO, June 2008: 58–59.

34. David L. Greene, Andreas Schafer, "Reducing Greenhouse Gas Emissions from U.S. Transportation," Pew Center on Global Climate Change, May 2003, http://www.pewclimate.org/docUploads/ustransp.pdf.

35. U.S. Department of Energy, Energy Information Administration, *Annual Energy Review 2005,* July 2006, Washington, D.C.: 380.

36. *New York City Tallies Its Greenhouse Gas Emissions,* Environmental News Service, April 11, 2007, http://www.ens-newswire.com/ens/apr2007/2007-04-11-03.asp.

Chapter 3: Greening the Organization

1. "Corporate Responsibility & Sustainability Communications: Who's Listening? Who's Leading? What Matters Most?," survey, Edelman Public Relations, May 2008. The survey included four hundred people in the United States, three hundred in China, and one hundred and fifty each in Brazil, Canada, France, Germany, India, Ireland, Italy, Japan, Mexico, the Netherlands, Poland, Russia, South Korea, Spain, Sweden, and the United Kingdom. The demographic profile of those interviewed in the 2007 survey is as follows: college-educated; 35 to 64 years of age; reporting a household income in the top quartile of their country; and reporting a significant interest in and engagement with the media, and economic and policy affairs.

2. Julie Garden (Real Estate Manager for Cisco Systems, Ltd.), in interview with the author, September 18, 2008.

3. Jay Boren and Omar Khan (Google.org), in interview with the author, November 12, 2008.

4. Michael Barbado, "At Wal-Mart, Lessons in Self-Help," *New York Times,* April 5, 2007, http://www.nytimes.com/2007/04/05/business/05improve.html?fta=y/.

5. Kevin Kampschroer (Acting Director, Office of Federal High-Performance Green Buildings with the U.S. General Services Administration), in interview with the author, August 14, 2008.

6. John Elkington, Cannibals with Forks: The Triple Bottom Line of 21st Century Business, (Oxford: Capstone Publishing Ltd., 1999), 69–94.

7. "Does Your Company Need a Chief Green Officer?," *Environmental Leader,* June 2007, http://www.environmentalleader.com/2007/06/12/does-your-company-need-a-chief-green-officer/.

8. Claudia Deutsch. "Companies Giving Green an Office," *New York Times,* July 3, 2007, http://www.nytimes.com/2007/07/03/business/03sustain.html.

9. Curtis Ravenel (Bloomberg's Head of Global Sustainable Initiatives), in interview with the author, October 31, 2007.

10. "GE ecomagination R&D Investment to Reach $1 Billion by Year End, Driving Expansion of Advanced Technology Pipeline," *Business Wire,* October 23, 2007, http://www.genewscenter.com/Content/Detail.asp?ReleaseID=2748&NewsAreaID=2.

11. Kevin Kampschroer (Acting Director, Office of Federal High-Performance Green Buildings for the U.S. General Services Administration), in interview with the author, August 14, 2008.

12. Meeta Shingne (Manager Real Estate, and Andy Hammond, Project Manager, for WPP Group), in interview with the author, August 27, 2008.

13. "Governor Schwarzenegger Announces Winners of Prestigious Environmental Awards: Winners Honored for Sustaining Economic Development While Protecting the Environment" (press release, California Environmental Protection Agency, December 1, 2003), http://www.calepa.ca.gov/PressRoom/Releases/2003/R6.htm.

14. "Whole Foods Market Provides $1 Million in Loans to Small-Scale Local Food Producers to Aid Growth" (press release, November 13, 2007), http://www.wholefoodsmarket.com/pressroom/2007/11/13/whole-foods-market-provides–1-million-in-loans-to-small-scale-local-food-producers-to-aid-growth/.

15. Whole Foods 2008 Stakeholder Report, http://www.wholefoodsmarket.com/company/pdfs/ar08.pdf.

Chapter 4: Your Green Road Map

1. Curtis Ravenel (Head of Global Sustainability Initiatives, Bloomberg), interview with the author, October 31, 2008.
2. Meeta Shingne (Real Estate Manager, the WPP Group), and Andy Hammond (Programme and Project Management, the WPP Group), interviews with the author, August 27, 2008.
3. The Sustainable Design and Energy Reduction Manual is posted for public use at the VA's Technical Information Library and is available online at http://www.va.gov/facmgt/standard/energy.asp.

Chapter 5: Encouraging Green Behavior

1. Thomas L. Friedman, *The World Is Flat* (New York: Farrar, Straus and Giroux, 2006), 13.
2. Malcolm Gladwell, *The Tipping Point* (Boston: Little, Brown and Company, 2000).
3. Robert B. Cialdini, "Don't Throw in the Towel: Use Social Influence Research," *Association for Psychological Science Observer,* 18, no. 4 (April 2005): 33–34.
4. Sandy Thomaes (Senior Consultant, Corporate Real Estate), in interview with the author, March 12, 2008.
5. The fair trade movement advocates the payment of a fair price as well as social and environmental standards related to the production of a wide variety of goods. It often refers to exports from developing countries to developed countries, especially handicrafts, coffee, cocoa, sugar, tea, bananas, honey, cotton, wine, fresh fruit, chocolate, and flowers.
6. Carbon Disclosure Project (CDP6) Questionnaire, survey, Carbon Disclosure Project, February, 2008. http://www.cdproject.net/CDP2008Questionnaire.asp.
7. Julie Garden (Real Estate Manager for Cisco Systems, Ltd.), in interview with the author, September 18, 2008.
8. Sandy Thomaes interview.
9. Randy Knox (Senior Director Global Workplace Solutions for Adobe Systems Inc.), in interview with the author, October 15, 2008.
10. Alicia Martin (Sustainability Manager for Sprint), in interview with the author, February 5, 2008.

Chapter 6: Green Recruiting

1. John Sullivan, "Green Recruiting: Building Your Environmental Employment Brand," *ere.net,* March 6, 2007, http://www.ere.net/2007/06/04/green-recruiting-building-your-environmental-employment-brand/.
2. Sullivan, "Green Recruiting."
3. The Conference Board, "Business Opportunity in Citizenship and Sustainability Issues Exist, but Few Can Capitalize" press release, November 9, 2006, http://www.conference-board.org/utilities/pressDetail.cfm?press_ID=3005/.
4. Addeco USA, "Earth Day 2007: Are American Workers Going Green?," press release, *harrisinteractive.com,* April 10, 2007, http://www.harrisinteractive.com/news/newsletters/clientnews/2007_Adecco.pdf/.
5. Justina Victor, "SHRM Survey Brief: Green Workplace," *Society for Human Resource Management,* January 2008, 2–4.

6. Charlotte Huff, "Green Recruiting Helps Bring in Top Talent," *Workforce Management,* August 2007, 2, www.workforce.com/archive/feature/25/06/24/index.php.

7. Justina Victor, "SHRM Survey Brief: Green Workplace."

8. "The Six Sins of Greenwashing," TerraChoice Environmental Marketing Inc., November, 2007, http://www.terrachoice.com/files/6_sins.pdf.

9. Kellie A. McElhaney, Michael W. Toffel, and Natalie Hill, "Designing Sustainability at BMW Group: The Designworks/USA Experience" (Working Paper Series, Haas School of Business, University of California, Berkeley, December, 2002), http://repositories.cdlib.org/crb/wps/4/.

10. Google says, 'Here Comes The Sun' Internet Giant To Run One Third of its Campus on Solar Power," *MSNBC.com,* October 17, 2006, http://www.msnbc.msn.com/id/15301514/.

11. I was the consultant hired to help Robertson Homes green their office along with Dell. For videos of our "makeover" go to: (1) http://tinyurl.com/c9ljrm and (2) http://tinyurl.com/ccbgk7.

12. Progressive Automotive X Prize Web site: http://www.progressiveautoxprize.org/

13. Kelly Spors, "Employee Benefits Go Green," *Wall Street Journal,* November 14, 2007, http://blogs.wsj.com/independentstreet/2007/11/14/employee-benefits-go-green/.

14. Huff, "Green Recruiting."

15. Justina Victor, "SHRM Survey Brief: Green Workplace."

Chapter 7: Leveraging Technology

1. Energy Star, Labeling Energy Efficient Office Equipment, "Desktop vs. Laptop," http://www.eu-energystar.org/en/en_022p.shtml.

2. Don Horn, AIA (Director, PBS Sustainability Program, Office of Federal High-Performance Green Buildings, GSA Public Buildings Service), in interview with the author, February 21, 2008.

3. Elizabeth Rosenthal, *China Increases Lead as Biggest Carbon Dioxide Emitter, New York Times,* June 14, 2008, http://www.nytimes.com/2008/06/14/world/asia/14china.html/.

4. Alicia Martin (Manager, Sustainability, Corporate Real Estate, Sprint), in interview with the author, February 5, 2008.

5. Don Tapscott and Anthony Williams, *Wikinomics: How Mass Collaboration Changes Everything* (New York: Penguin Group 2006), 39.

6. Colin Stewart, "Second Life as a Simulation Tool," *Orange County Register,* December 2007.

7. Jessica Bennett, "Power in Numbers: How Wiki Software Is Reforming Bloated Bureaucracies and Changing the Face of Communication," *Newsweek,* August 2007, http://www.newsweek.com/id/32711.

8. Editorial, *"Pay-as-You-Drive Auto Insurance,"* LA *Los Angeles Times,* August 29, 2008, http://www.latimes.com/news/opinion/la-ed-insurance29-2008aug29,0,4558879.story.

9. John E. Petersen, Vladislav Shunturov, Kathryn Janda, Gavin Platt, and Kate Weinberger, "Dormitory Residents Reduce Electricity Consumption When Exposed to Real-Time Visual Feedback And Incentives," *International Journal of Sustainability in Higher Education,* 8, no. 1 (2007): 16–33.

10. Alex Wilson, "Energy Dashboards: Using Real-Time Feedback to Influence Behavior," BuildingGreen.com, December 1, 2008, http://www.buildinggreen.com/auth/

article.cfm/2008/11/24/Energy-Dashboards-Using-Real-Time-Feedback-to-Influence-Behavior.

11.   Robert L. Mitchell, "The Rise of Smart Buildings," *Computer World,* March 14, 2005.

12.   Various authors, "Integrated Project Delivery: A Guide," *American Institute of Architects,* 1 (2007): 10–17.

13.   Wade Roush, "PeopleCube Says Office Scheduling Software Can Slow Global Warming," *Xconomy,* March 10, 2008.

14.   Frank Bick (Executive Vice President and Chief Financial Officer, The Bick Group), in interview with the author, June 1, 2007.

15.   Katie Fehrenbacher, "GridPoint Raises Massive $120M, Grabs Plug-In Startup V2Green," *earth2tech,* September 23, 2008, http://earth2tech.com/2008/09/23/grid-point-raises-massive–120m-grabs-plug-in-startup-v2green/.

16.   Justin Moresco, "GridPoint Gets $15M and Big-Name Advisers," *Red Herring,* March 28, 2008, http://www.redherring.com/Home/24040.

Chapter 8: Greening Operations

1.   Interface Vision Statement from Interface Website, http://www.interfaceglobal.com/Company/Mission-Vision.aspx.

2.   Georgia Institute of Technology, School of Industrial and Systems Engineering, "Nature and the Industrial Enterprise: Mid-Course Correction," *Engineering Enterprise,* Georgia Institute of Technology (Spring 2004), p. 7, http://hdl.handle.net/1853/7376/.

3.   "Green Auditing," *GreenBiz.com,* December 2, 2003, http://www.greenbiz.com/resources/resource/green-auditing/.

4.   Randy Knox (Adobe Systems Inc.), in interview with the author, October 15, 2008.

5.   Sarah Anderson and John Cavanagh, "Top 200: The Rise of Corporate Global Power," Institute for Policy Studies, December 4, 2000.

6.   Alicia Martin (Manager, Sustainability, Sprint), in interview with the author, February 5, 2008.

7.   Peter Johnston (Boston Properties), in interview with the author, July 21, 2008.

8.   The National Institute of Standards and Technology (NIST) Handbook 135, 1995 edition, defines Life Cycle Cost (LCC) as "the total discounted dollar cost of owning, operating, maintaining, and disposing of a building or a building system" over a period of time. Life Cycle Cost Analysis (LCCA) is an economic evaluation technique that determines the total cost of owning and operating a facility over period of time.

9.   Sandy Thomaes (Senior Consultant, Corporate Real Estate), in interview with the author, March 12, 2008.

10.   Rogelio Oliva and James Quinn, "Interface's Evergreen Services Agreement," *Harvard Business Review* Case Study, February 25, 2003.

11.   John Murawski, *Burt's Bees Backs Offsets, News and Observer,* March 2, 2008, http://www.newsobserver.com/print/sunday/work_money/story/976740.html.

12.   Peter Johnston, (Senior Vice President and Regional Manager for Boston Properties), in interview with the author, July 21, 2008.interview.

13.   Stacy Feldman, "UPS Goes on Left-Turn Diet, Slims Down Its Carbon Footprint," *Solve Climate,* April 22, 2008, http://solveclimate.com/blog/20080422/ups-goes-left-turn-diet-slims-down-its-carbon-footprint/.

14.   William McDonough and Michael Braungart, *Cradle to Cradle: Remaking the Way We Make Things* (New York: North Point Press, 2002), 92.

15. Information on Anheuser-Busch taken from the Environmental Protection Agency (EPA) Web site at http://www.epa.gov/epawaste/partnerships/wastewise/success/xlarge.htm/.

16. Information on Walt Disney Studios taken from the EPA Web site, at http://www.epa.gov/epawaste/partnerships/wastewise/success/xlarge.htm/.

17. Mark Gunther, "The End of Garbage," *Fortune,* March 14, 2007, http://money.cnn.com/magazines/fortune/fortune_archive/2007/03/19/8402369/index.htm/.

18. Ibid.

19. "Electronic Product Management Issues" are published by the California Integrated Waste Management Board, February 2002, http://www.ciwmb.ca.gov/Publications/BizWaste/44102002.pdf.

20. The EIA Consumer Education Initiative, or "CEI," is a Web-based information resource that provides consumers and others with information on recycling and reuse opportunities for used electronics. Participating manufacturers include an industry statement in a variety of media, including owner's manuals, company Web sites, and product literature, directing consumers to the CEI Web page where consumers can find recycling and reuse opportunities for used electronics in their area.

21. P. J. Wade, "Innovation Frontier: Canadian District Energy & Deep Water Cooling," *Realty Times,* September 2006, http://realtytimes.com/rtpages/20060912_deepwater.htm.

22. Kellie A. McElhaney, Michael W. Toffel, and Natalie Hill, "Designing Sustainability at BMW Group: The Designworks/USA Experience" (Working Paper Series, Haas School of Business, University of California, Berkeley, December 2002), http://repositories.cdlib.org/crb/wps/4/.

Chapter 9: Transformative Design

1. Herbert Simon, *The Sciences of the Artificial, Second Edition* (Massachusetts Institute of Technology, 1996), p. xii.

2. Roger Martin, *The Design of Business,* Joseph L. Rotman School of Management, Winter 2004, p. 10.

3. Jennifer Kho, "Reincarnation for Paper, Without Recycling," Green Tech Media, May 2, 2008, http://www.greentechmedia.com/articles/reincarnation-for-paper-without-recycling–862.html/.

4. Jeanne Liedtka, "Strategy as Design," *Rotman Management* Winter 2004, 12–15.

5. Data taken from the Vertical Farm Project Website, http://www.verticalfarm.com/.

6. Data taken from the Biomimicry Institute Website, http://www.biomimicryinstitute.org/.

7. Roseliek van de Velden, "Using Awareness in Product Design to Influence Sustainable Behaviour" (Working Paper, Department of Product Design, Norwegian University of Science and Technology, 2003), http://www.ivt.ntnu.no/ipd/docs/pd9_2003/Velden.pdf.

8. S. R. Kellert, J. H. Heerwagen, and M. Mador, eds., *Biophilic Design: Theory, Science and Practice* (New Jersey: John Wiley & Sons, Inc., 2008).

9. Judith H. Heerwagen, "Investing In People: The Social Benefits of Sustainable Design," (Working Paper, Rethinking Sustainable Construction'06, Sarasota, FL Conference, September, 2006, http://74.125.93.104/search?q=cache:xScIqta2SOwJ:courses.caup.washington.edu/ARCH/498C/JHInvestinginPeople.doc+Investing+In+People:+The+Social+Benefits+of+Sustainable+Design+heerwagen&cd=6&hl=en&ct=clnk&gl=us.

10.   L. Heschong, "Windows and Office Worker Performance: The SMUD Call Center and Desktop Studies," in D. Clements-Croome (ed.), *Creating the Productive Workplace,* 2nd ed. (New York: Taylor & Francis), pp. 277–309.

11.   Heerwagen, "Investing in People."

12.   Ibid.

13.   R. Cooper, "The Psychology of Boredom, *Science Journal* 4, no. 2 (1968): 38–42.

14.   The workstations used in this insurance company study, referred to as "environmentally responsive workstations" or ERWs, integrate and provide heating, cooling, lighting, ventilation and other environmental qualities directly to the occupants of workstations. They key feature of the ERW is that the occupant controls, modulates and maintains the environmental conditions.

15.   W. Kroner, J. A. Stark-Martin, T. Willemain, "Using Advanced Office Technology to Increase Productivity" (Working Paper, Rensselaer Polytechnic Institute: Center for Architectural Research, 1992).

16.   American Society of Heating, Refrigeration and Air-conditioning Engineers (ASHRAE), Chapter 9: Indoor Environmental Health, Table 1, January 1, 2005.

17.   Gram-negative bacteria are those bacteria that do not retain crystal violet dye in the gram staining protocol. Many species of gram-negative bacteria are pathogenic, meaning they can cause disease in a host organism. This pathogenic capability is usually associated with certain components of gram-negative cell walls, in particular the lipopolysaccharide (also known as LPS or endotoxin) layer. In humans, LPS triggers an innate immune response characterized by cytokine production and immune system activation. Inflammation is a common result of cytokine production, which can also produce host toxicity.

18.   A. Kjellberg, U. Landstrom, M. Tesarz, L. Soderberg, and E. Akerlund, "The Effects Of Nonphysical Noise Characteristics, Ongoing Task and Noise Sensitivity on Annoyance and Distraction Due to Noise at Work," *Journal of Environmental Psychology,* 16 (1996): 123–136.

19.   Heerwagen, "Investing in People."

20.   F. R. H. Zijlstra, R. A. Roe, A. B. Leonora, and I. Krediet, "Temporal Factors in Mental Work: Effects of Interrupted Activities," *Journal of Occupational and Organizational Psychology,* 72 (1999): 163–185.

Chapter 10: Changing When, Where, and How You Work

1.   Someone who is employed due to his or her knowledge of a subject matter, rather than their ability to perform manual labor.

2.   Associated Press, "Utah is Going to a 4-Day Work Week: In an Effort to Save Energy, State Employees Will Get Friday Off," *MSNBC.com,* July 3, 2008, http://www.msnbc.msn.com/id/25518225/.

3.   Kevin Kelly (Senior Architect, Work Space Delivery Program, General Services Administration, Public Building Service), in interview with the author, March 14, 2008.

4.   Ron Zemke, Claire Raines, and Bob Filipczak, *Generations at Work* (New York: AMACOM, 2000).

5.   Judith Heerwagen (Founder, PhD, J.H. Heerwagen Associates), in interview with the author, August 26, 2008.

6.   Kevin Kelly interview.

7.   David Dunn (Workplace Planning, Real Estate and Construction, Nortel Real Estate), in interview with the author, October 5, 2008.

8. Julie Garden (Cisco, Bedfont Lakes, UK), in interview with the author, September 18, 2008.

9. U.S. Census Bureau, "Americans Spend More Than 100 Hours Commuting to Work Each Year, Census Bureau Reports," March 30, 2005, http://www.census.gov/Press-Release/www/releases/archives/american_community_survey_acs/004489.html.

10. U.S. Census Bureau, "Most of Us Still Drive to Work—Alone," June 13, 2007, http://www.census.gov/Press-Release/www/releases/archives/american_community_survey_acs/010230.html.

11. Alex Wilson and Rachel Navaro, "Driving to Green Buildings: The Transportation Energy Intensity of Buildings," *Environmental Building News,* September 1, 2007, http://www.buildinggreen.com/auth/article.cfm?fileName=160901a.xml/.

12. Eve Tahmincioglu, "Why the Lunch Break Is Going Extinct: More Workers Are Told to Multi-Task as They Wolf Down Food," *MSNBC.com,* August 20, 2007, http://www msnbc.msn.com/id/20265063/.

13. Sasha Talcott, "Incentives Come Nonstop for Buyers of Hybrids," *Bostonglobe.com,* June 7, 2006, http://www.boston.com/business/articles/2006/06/07/incentives_come _nonstop_for_buyers_of_hybrids/.

14. Ben Mack, "Cars with More Emissions Pay Bigger Parking Fees in Britain," *Wired,* January 8, 2009, http://blog.wired.com/cars/2009/01/great-britain-u.html/.

15. Paul Westbrook (Sustainable Development Manager, Texas Instruments), in interview with the author, August 26, 2008.

Chapter 11: The Green Workplace of the Future

1. Facts from a video by Karl Fisch, Scott McLeod, and Jeff Brenman, http://www .youtube.com/watch?v=jpEnFwiqdx8.

2. Alan Greenspan (speech), von der Mehden Hall, University of Connecticut, October 14, 1997.

3. Alan Greenspan, "The Critical Role of Education in the Nation's Economy" (remarks, Greater Omaha Chamber of Commerce Annual Meeting, Omaha, Nebraska, February 20, 2004).

4. Bill Valentine (Chairman, HOK Group), in interview with the author, August 22, 2008.

5. Judith Heerwagen (Founder, PhD, J. H. Heerwagen Associates), in interview with the author, August 26, 2008.

6. Chris Hood (Program Manager, Hewlett Packard's Workplace), in interview with the author, March 24, 2008.

7. Chris Hood interview.

8. Kevin Kelly (AIA, Senior Architect, Work Space Delivery Program, General Services Administration, Public Building Service), in interview with the author, March 14, 2008.

9. David Dunn (Workplace Planning, Innovation and Construction, Nortel Real Estate), in interview with the author, October 5, 2008.

10. Randy Knox (Senior Director, Global Workplace Solutions, Adobe Systems Inc.), in interview with the author, October 15, 2008.

11. *Global Trends in Sustainable Energy Investment, 2008: Analysis of Trends and Issues in the Financing of Renewable Energy and Energy Efficiency,* United Nations Environment Programme and New Energy Finance, 2008.

12. Greenbiz Staff, "LOHAS Forum Sees Big Growth in Green Marketplace," May 30, 2007, http://greenbiz.com/news/2007/05/30/lohas-forum-sees-big-growth-green-marketplace.

13.   Joel Makower, "State of Green Business 2008," greenbiz.com, January 30, 2008, http://www.greenbiz.com/blog/2008/01/30/the-state-green-business-2008/.

14.   "Change in Energy and Commerce Committee Leadership Will Effect Energy Sector," *Energy Business Daily*, December 16, 2008, http://energybusinessdaily.com/renewables/change-in-energy-and-commerce-committee-leadership-will-effect-energy-sector/.

15.   Jeff Austin (Senior VP of Sustainability Strategies, Wachovia Corp.), in interview with the author, March 25, 2008.

16.   Jeff Austin (Senior VP of Sustainability Strategies, Wachovia Corp.), in interview with the author, March 25, 2008.

17.   Chris Hood interview.

Index